BACON AND SHAKESPEARE

LECTOR HOUSE PUBLIC DOMAIN WORKS

This book is a result of an effort made by Lector House towards making a contribution to the preservation and repair of original classic literature. The original text is in the public domain in the United States of America, and possibly other countries depending upon their specific copyright laws.

In an attempt to preserve, improve and recreate the original content, certain conventional norms with regard to typographical mistakes, hyphenations, punctuations and/or other related subject matters, have been corrected upon our consideration. However, few such imperfections might not have been rectified as they were inherited and preserved from the original content to maintain the authenticity and construct, relevant to the work. The work might contain a few prior copyright references which have been retained, wherever considered relevant to the part of the construct. We believe that this work holds historical, cultural and/or intellectual importance in the literary works community, therefore despite the oddities, we accounted the work for print as a part of our continuing effort towards preservation of literary work and our contribution towards the development of the society as a whole, driven by our beliefs.

We are grateful to our readers for putting their faith in us and accepting our imperfections with regard to preservation of the historical content. We shall strive hard to meet up to the expectations to improve further to provide an enriching reading experience.

Though, we conduct extensive research in ascertaining the status of copyright before redeveloping a version of the content, in rare cases, a classic work might be incorrectly marked as not-in-copyright. In such cases, if you are the copyright holder, then kindly contact us or write to us, and we shall get back to you with an immediate course of action.

HAPPY READING!

BACON AND SHAKESPEARE

ALBERT FREDERICK CALVERT

ISBN: 978-93-90294-32-9

Published: -

© 2020
LECTOR HOUSE LLP

LECTOR HOUSE LLP
E-MAIL: lectorpublishing@gmail.com

FRANCIS BACON. FROM A MINIATURE BY PETER OLIVER.
belonging to His Grace the Duke of Buccleuch.

BACON AND SHAKESPEARE.

BY

ALBERT F. CALVERT.

1902.

PREFACE.

To anticipate for this little book that it may prove the means of convincing a single Baconian of the error of his ways, would be to express a hope that has only the faintest chance of realisation. Baconianism is so wilful and so obstinate that it is not amenable to any treatment that has yet been invented. It has its root in an entire misconception of the character and temperament of the man Bacon; it is nourished on the grossest misrepresentation of the man Shakespeare that the memory of an author has ever been subjected to. So long as the fallacy, backed up by specious argument, was confined to the consideration of the mighty few, it was scarcely necessary to enter into the lists with the Baconian champions, but the new and energetic move which is now being made to cast down Shakespeare from the "topmost pinnacle in the temple of fame," and to set up the figure of Bacon in his stead, has had the result of bringing the subject once more into public view. In the circumstances, the publication of the following summary of the evidence may be found not inopportune. It may not effect a cure in the case of confirmed Baconians, but I have a modest hope that it will enable the unprejudiced inquirer to be on his guard against the hallucination. The Baconians have woven a cunning mesh of fact and fable to entangle the mind of the unwary; the task I have set myself is to review the premises, test the arguments, and combat the conclusions upon which Bacon's pretensions to the authorship of Shakespeare's plays is alleged to rest, and to explain the reasons that we hold for ascribing the authorship of the Plays to Shakespeare.

While the majority of Shakespearean students are impatient of discussion, the disciples of the Baconian theory are prompt and eager and voluminous in the propagation of their arguments. Indeed, they have, all along, had the lion's share in the controversy, and by their much speaking, have stormed the ears of that section of the public which neither thinks for itself, nor will be at the trouble to verify what it is told. Bacon has been born again in the biographies of his devotees, and Shakespeare, by the same agency, has been edited out of recognition. Bacon's brilliant intellectual qualities have been taken as the basis of all argument, the human and temperamental side of his character has been boldly made amenable to the exigencies of argument, and his many glaringly reprehensible actions have been carefully ignored. I have endeavoured, in the ensuing pages, not so much to give a picture of the complete man, as to show what he was capable of in the way of selfishness, trickery and subterfuge. He was capable of the basest ingratitude and meanness, of the employment of barbarity when it suited his purpose, of unctuous servility and boundless egoism. He had neither the temperament nor the poetical ability nor the time to write the Plays; had he the meanness of spirit to claim them as his own? We shall see!

The conclusions I have formed with respect to the two cipher revelations which are now agitating the minds of both Shakespeareans and Baconians are derived partly from my estimate of the character of Bacon, partly from the apparent sincerity of Mrs. Gallup, and

PREFACE.

partly again from what I know of other and entirely independent decipherations of further Bacon messages, which are now being actively made in this country. Of Mrs. Gallup I only know that which her book and her publishers reveal. Of Dr. Orville W. Owen, the discoverer of the word-cipher I learn, from an American source, quoted by way of a testimonial in one of the doctor's books, that he is "a man who has reached middle age," and who has "never shown the slightest sign of possessing unusual or extraordinary literary skill, or genius." In other words, his sponsors assure us that he is incapable of writing those portions of Shakespeare which form so great a part of his decipherations, or even the connecting passages which appear to have been contributed by Bacon. We must accept this opinion as a tribute of personal character.

Concerning the illustrations, I may be allowed to say a few explanatory words. The two photogravure reproductions are taken respectively from a miniature by Peter Oliver, belonging to the Duke of Buccleuch, and from a very rare print of Bacon. The print from Vansomer's painting, the picture of Bacon's monument, and the portraits of Sir Nicholas Bacon, Sir Nathaniel Bacon, the Earl of Essex and Queen Elizabeth, and the views of Stratford-on-Avon and Gorhambury will, I trust, be found of general interest. The facsimile pages from "Sylva Sylvarum" and the "Novum Organum," with their allegorical devises and fine workmanship, illustrate the contrast between the manner in which the works of Bacon and those of Shakespeare were given to the world. The portraits of Shakespeare contained here are well known to students. The reproduction of the bust will be familiar to all visitors to Stratford, the "Droeshout" Engraving is the picture which forms the frontispiece to the First Folio, and the original of the Chandos portrait is now in the National Portrait Gallery.

Albert F. Calvert.

"Royston," Eton Avenue,
London, N.W.

CONTENTS

		Page
	Preface.	vi
I.	Bacon, the Product of His Age.	1
II.	Bacon, the Friend of Essex and Cecil.	6
III.	Bacon as the Creature of Buckingham.	12
IV.	Bacon and Shakespeare Contrasted.	18
V.	Baconian Fallacies Respecting Shakespeare.	20
VI.	Mr. Theobald, a Baconian by Intuition.	24
VII.	Was Shakespeare the "Upstart Crow?"	27
VIII.	Wm. Shakespeare, Money Lender and Poet.	31
IX.	The "True Shakespeare."	34
X.	Mr. Theobald's Parallels and Mr. Bayley's Conclusions.	38
XI.	The Bi-Literal Cipher.	43
XII.	Bacon's "Sterne and Tragicle History."	50
XIII.	Bacon, the Author of all Elizabethan-Jacobean Literature.	55
XIV.	Bacon and "Divine Aide."	63
XV.	Shakespeare and Bacon in Collaboration.	66
XVI.	The Tragical Historie of our Late Brother Robert, Earl of Essex.	71
XVII.	Bacon, the Poet.	77
XVIII.	"Did Shakespeare Write Bacon?"	80
XIX.	The Case for Shakespeare.	83

CONTENTS

XX. Were Shakespeare and Bacon Acquainted?. 89

XXI. In Conclusion. 92

LIST OF ILLUSTRATIONS

Page

I. Francis Bacon. From A Miniature By Peter Oliver.. iv
II. Francis Bacon. Aged 18. 1578. From A Miniature By Hilliard. 3
III. Francis Bacon As Lord Chancellor (Vansomer) 8
IV. Francis Bacon As Lord Chancellor. 11
V. The Monument Of Lord Bacon In St. Michael's Church. 14
VI. Sir Nicholas Bacon. 17
VII. Anna Lady Bacon, Mother Of Francis Bacon. 22
VIII. Sir Nathaniel Bacon.. 25
IX. St. Michael's Church. 29
X. Elizabeth R 32
XI. Robert Devereux, Earl Of Essex. O.b. 1601. 36
XII. Robert Dudley, Earl Of Leicester. 39
XIII. Frontispiece To Sylva Sylvarum 42
XIV. Frontispiece To Novum Organum. 48
XV. Gorhambury, A.d. 1568.. 51
XVI. Gorhambury, A.d. 1795.. 51
XVII. Gorhambury, A.d. 1821.. 51
XVIII. Shakespeare. The Droeshout Etching, ... 57
XIX. Shakespeare. The Chandos Portrait.. 60
XX. The Bust Of Shakespeare At Stratford-On-Avon. 69

LIST OF ILLUSTRATIONS

XXI. Shakespeare's House. 78

XXII. The Chancel Of Trinity Church, Stratford-On-Avon. 81

XXIII. Shakespeare Autographs 84

XXIV. Ann Hathaway's Cottage At Shottery.. 87

XXV. Dr. Owen's Wheel For Deciphering 91

BACON & SHAKESPEARE.

BACON, THE PRODUCT OF HIS AGE.

It is impossible to sympathise with, or even to regard seriously, the spirit in which a small, but growing section of the reading public of America, and of this country, has plunged into the controversy respecting the authorship of the so-called Shakespeare plays. The fantastic doubt which compelled individual scholars to investigate a theory of their own inventing, to lay, so to speak, the ghost they had themselves raised, has inspired distrust in the minds that had no beliefs, and generated scepticism in those where no faith was. The search for the truth has degenerated into a wild-goose chase; the seekers after some new thing have made the quest their own; ignorance has plagiarised from prejudice; the "grand old Bacon-Shakespeare controversy," as Whistler said of Art, is upon the town—"to be chucked under the chin by the passing gallant—to be enticed within the gates of the householder—to be coaxed into company as a proof of culture and refinement." The difficulties that such a controversy present to the tea-table oracles are both numerous, and exceeding obstinate. The people who read Shakespeare form a pitiably insignificant proportion of the community, but they are multitudinous compared with those who have the remotest acquaintance with the works of Francis Bacon. Bacon is known to some as Elizabeth's little Lord Keeper, to others his name recalls the fact that he was James the First's Lord Chancellor, but outside his *Essays*, and, perhaps, *The New Atlantis*, his great philosophical dissertations, the pride and treasure which he so carefully preserved in Latin, lest they should be lost in the decay of modern languages, are a sealed book to all, except a few odd scholars at the Universities. Bacon is an extinct volcano. The fact is not creditable to the culture of the age, but it is incontrovertible.

It has, on this account, been found necessary for Baconians to describe to their readers what manner of man this was whom they would perch on Shakespeare's pedestal, and they have accomplished their task in the manner best calculated to lend plausibility to their theories. Moreover, they have displayed a subtle appreciation of the magnitude of their undertaking. The Shakespeare plays, in common with all great works, reflect in some degree the personality of their creator. The Baconian students cannot deny that there are many characteristics in their candidate which only the most devout can reconcile with the spirit of the plays. It, therefore, became further necessary to ring the changes on their candidate; to employ the arguments of induction and deduction as best suited the exigencies of the task. In creating the idol of Bacon, much had to be read into the subject, and it would seem that the simplest method by which they could advance the claims of Bacon was by discrediting the claims of Shakespeare. In estimating the character of Viscount St. Alban, we have the solid foundation of fact for our guidance; the personal details of Shakespeare's career may be written upon a page of note paper. The original Baconians seized upon these few details to distort them to their own ends, and their followers have done their best to perpetuate the outrage.

In the scope of this volume it is not possible, nor is it necessary, to attempt an intimate analysis of the characters of Bacon and Shakespeare, but a resumé of the leading incidents in their lives, a brief review for the purpose of making a comparison of their respective temperaments, will not be out of place. In the following pages my endeavour has been to arrange, as systematically as possible, the reasons for my belief—for these I invite a courteous hearing; as for the conclusions I have formed, I am content to abide by them.

My last desire in dealing with the career of Lord Bacon has been to find reasons for supposing him to be the author of Shakespeare's plays. That endeavour has been made by his many champions with more sanguinity than I could display, and I have carefully weighed every argument and fact advanced in his favour. I have read, and re-read, and argued against myself, the claims which have been put forward with so much earnestness and evident conviction. But against these I have had to set the bald facts that make the claim untenable. The biographers of Bacon have been burdened with the ungrateful necessity of finding excuses, and of making endless apologies for their hero. Bacon's greatest editor, the scholar who devoted some 30 years to the work—who brought more knowledge, and disclosed more analytical acumen and skilled judgment in his task than any editor ever brought to bear upon the life and works of a single author—has stated his reasons for his disbelief in the Baconian theory. When it is remembered that Spedding's knowledge of Shakespeare was "extensive and profound, and his laborious and subtle criticism derived additional value from his love of the stage," his decision on the subject must be accepted, if not as incontrovertible, at least, as the most damaging blow to the Baconian theory we shall ever get.

A well-known writer, in declaring that a man's morality has nothing to do with his prose, perpetrated an aphorism which Baconians have adduced to reconcile the psychological differences which we find between Bacon, the man, and Bacon, the author of the plays traditionally attributed to Shakespeare. The least erudite student of Shakespeare has felt the magic of the dramatist's boundless sympathy, his glowing imagination, his gentleness, truth and simplicity. His mind, as Hazlitt recognised, contained within itself the germs of all faculty and feeling, and Mr. Sidney Lee, in his general estimate of Shakespeare's genius, has written, "In knowledge of human nature, in wealth of humour, in depth of passion, in fertility of fancy, and in soundness of judgment, he has not a rival." Henry Chettle refers to "his uprightness of dealing which argues his honesty," the author of *The Return from Parnassus* apostrophised him as "sweet Master Shakespeare," and Ben Jonson, his friend and fellow labourer, wrote of him, "I loved the man, and do honour his memory, on this side idolatry as much as any. He was indeed honest, and of an open and free nature."

FRANCIS BACON. AGED 18. 1578. FROM A MINIATURE BY HILLIARD.

An author's morality, or rather his lack of it, may not detract from the grace and clarity of his style, but it must inevitably leave its mark in his matter. There is poetry that reveals only the brilliance of the writer's brain—if such can be termed poetry; there is prose which lays bare the writer's heart. In Shakespeare we have verse which evidences the possession of both the mental and the temperamental qualities in the highest perfection. There is Shakespeare the genius, the artist, the creator, the master manipulator of theatrical machinery. There is Shakespeare the man—the citizen of whom Jonson wrote in terms of the warmest affection. In what degree do we find these qualities which are inseparably associated with Shakespeare in the character of Francis Bacon?

For every act of Bacon's life we are met with apologies, explanations, and extravagant defences. Lord Macaulay's bitter and brilliant analysis of the Lord Chancellor (a retaliatory treatise prompted by the ingenuity and perversions of his enamoured champions), has been robbed of its sting by the less brilliant, but more knowledgable and judicious Spedding, who in his *Evenings with a Reviewer*, clearly and dispassionately reduces Macaulay's estimate to its correct biographical and critical level. But there are acts in the life of Bacon that, shorn of all the swaddling clothes of specious explanation, reveal the man in a light which, in spite of valiant speculation and portentous argument, in spite even of Bacon's sworn word, render his claims to the mantle of Shakespeare an absurdity—and an impertinence.

Francis Bacon, the youngest son of Sir Nicholas Bacon, Lord Keeper of the Great Seal, by his second wife (Ann, daughter of Sir Anthony Coke), was born on 22nd January, 1561. He was the product of the age in which he lived. A politician by heredity, a student by nature, a courtier and place-seeker by force of circumstances, he fulfilled his inevitable destiny. In a court in which the politics were based on the teachings of Machiavelli, in which intrigue was a sport and a fine art, where flattery and lying were necessities, and personal advancement the one incentive to every act, Bacon intrigued, supplicated, flattered, cringed, and lied himself into prominence. Nor must the future Lord Chancellor be judged too harshly on that account. He was only gambling with the current coin of his environment. By nature, he was averse to Jesuitry, but he was forced by circumstances and his ambitions to employ it. "What the art of oratory was in democratic Athens," Dr. Edwin A. Abbott writes, "that the art of lying and flattery was for a courtier in the latter part of the Elizabethan monarchy." In this atmosphere of falseness and deception Bacon, with good credentials, a fine intellect, little money, many influential acquaintances, but few true friends, had to battle for his own fortunes. It is evident that he early recognised the exigencies of the warfare. He absorbed and assimilated the poison of his surroundings; he was both malleable and inventive. His frame of mind is best illustrated by two of his maxims. Truth, he declares is noble, and falsehood is base; yet "mixture of falsehood is like alloy in the coin of gold and silver, which may make the metal work the better." Again, "The best composition and temperament is to have openness in fame and opinion, secrecy in habit, dissimulation in seasonable use, and a power to feign if there be no remedy."

In the Elizabethan Court, the man who desired preferment had to plead for it. At the age of 16, Francis Bacon, after leaving Cambridge, had been admitted as "an ancient" of Gray's Inn, and in the following year was sent to Paris in the suite of Sir Amias Paulet, the English Ambassador. Two years later, on the death of his father, he returned to England, to find himself destitute of the patrimony he had expected to inherit, and forced to select the alternative of immediate work or the accumulation of debts. In this emergency he applied to his uncle, Lord Burghley, for advancement, and attempted to win the favour of the Queen by addressing to her a treatise entitled, *Advice to Queen Elizabeth*. This letter is remarkable for its lofty tone, its statesmanship, and boldness, but it is marred by the appendix, in which the author states that he is bold to entertain his opinions, "till I think that you think otherwise." This fatal pliancy, this note of excessive obsequiousness, lasted him through life.

The want of success, which attended his first efforts to gain official recognition, caused Bacon to decide, once and for all, upon his choice of a career. His path lay either in the way of politics, which meant preferment, power, and wealth; or science, philosophy, and the development of the arts and inventions that tend to civilise the life of man. No work seemed to him so meritorious as the latter, and for this he considered himself best adapted. "Whereas, I believe myself born for the service of mankind," he declared, in 1603, in the preface to *The Interpretation of Nature*; and in a letter to Lord Treasurer Burghley, "I have taken all knowledge to be my province." Again, "I found in my own nature a special adaptation for the contemplation of truth.... Imposture in every shape I utterly detested." But, as he proceeds to explain, "my birth, my rearing, and education," pointed not towards philosophy, but towards "politics;" love of truth and detestation of imposture was in his heart, but "the power to feign if there be no remedy" was there engraved also; the practical value of the "mixture of falsehood" was in his blood. And the want of money influenced him in forming his decision. In 1621, when his public career came to its disgraceful close, he declared that his greatest sin had been his desertion of philosophy and his having allowed himself to be diverted into politics. "Besides my innumerable sins," he cries out in his confession to the "Searcher of Souls," "I confess before Thee that I am debtor to Thee for the gracious talent of Thy gifts and graces, which I have neither put into a napkin, nor put it as I ought to exchangers, where it might have made most profit; but misspent it in things for which I was least fit, so that I may truly say, my soul has been a stranger in the course of my pilgrimage." At the beginning of his history, Bacon pleads his birth, his rearing and education as excuses for his choice of a career, and at its close, in *De Augmentis*, he throws the blame on "destiny" for carrying him into a political vortex. Dr. Abbott sums up his life-story in a phrase—*multum incola*; with it his public career began and ended.

BACON, THE FRIEND OF ESSEX AND CECIL.

HAVING failed to secure the goodwill of Burghley, Bacon addressed himself to the Earl of Essex, and when, in 1593, Francis came under the Queen's displeasure, Essex pleaded for his re-instatement in the Royal favour. Bacon himself practised every abasement, and, ever failing, debased himself to what he himself described as an exquisite disgrace. From this time until the day when there were "none so poor to do him reverence," the Earl of Essex was Bacon's warm friend, patron, and benefactor. He tided him over his monetary difficulties, made him his counsellor, and among other gifts presented him with a piece of land worth between £7,000 and £8,000. Bacon repaid his friendship with advice, which, it may be presumed, was well meant. But Bacon, the alleged author of the plays which portray an unrivalled knowledge of human nature, betrayed a singular and unaccountable lack of intuition into character. His counsel was, in a large measure, sound and sagacious, but it was utterly spoiled by the trickiness which breathes through every precept. If Bacon had possessed the knowledge of men that we find in Shakespeare, he would have known that his maxims were peculiarly unfit for Essex, who was the last man in the world to carry into effect such a scheme of systematic dissimulation. Dr. Abbott considers that few things did the Earl more harm than that the friend in whom he placed most trust gave him advice that was rather cunning than wise. Indeed, Essex was following the counsel of Bacon when he offered himself, in 1599, for the command in Ireland. From this command he returned to England a disgraced man, and his downfall culminated in his death two years later. And in the hour of his humiliation and dire need, when the Royal disfavour kept all his friends from him, Bacon's elder brother, Sir Anthony Bacon, and the author of the Sidney papers regarded Bacon as one of the active enemies of his former patron.

Bacon's biographers have strained every effort in explaining and excusing his action in the ensuing trials. Not only have they failed to exculpate him, but themselves must realise the futility of their most ingenious endeavours to clear his character of this foul blot. Abbott, his impartial biographer, says: "We may acquit him of everything but a cold-blooded indifference to his friend's interest and a supreme desire to pose (even at a friend's cost) as a loyal and much-persecuted servant of the Queen." But, truly, the most that can be said in extenuation of his behaviour, is little indeed, when the friend is a man to whom he had written, "I do think myself more beholding to you than to any man."

What, however, are the facts? When the first proceedings were taken against Essex in the Star Chamber, Bacon absented himself from the Court, his excuse to the Queen being, he said, "Some indisposition of body." His actual letter to Elizabeth explains that his absence was compelled by threats of violence on the part of the Earl's followers, whom he openly charges with a purpose to take the Queen's life. "My life has been threatened, and my name libelled. But these are the practices of those ... that would put out all your Majesty's lights, and fall on reckoning how many years you have reigned." Abbott considers that we need not accuse Bacon of deliberately intending by these words to poison the Queen's mind against his former friend, while Professor Gardiner adduces this imputation as a proof that Bacon was liable to "occasional ill-temper." Contemporary judgment did not so interpret the wording of the excuse. The treacherous nature of the insinuation provoked a feeling of amazement and anger. That his brother Anthony believed Bacon to be capable of so great vileness is evident, and even Lord Cecil, the Earl's greatest enemy, wrote to Francis begging him to be, as he himself was, "merely passive, and not active," in insuring the fallen Favourite's utter ruin.

In the face of these warnings and remonstrances, Bacon wrote to the Queen expressing his desire to serve her in the second stage of the proceedings against Essex. He asked that an important rôle might be assigned to him, but although he was only entrusted with a subsidiary part, he performed his task so adroitly as to earn the deep resentment of the friends of Essex. Within a fortnight of the Earl's liberation Bacon again offered his services to Essex, who accepted them!

What followed? Bacon devised a plan to secure the Earl's re-instatement in the Royal favour. The artifice employed was to bring before the notice of Elizabeth, a correspondence—ostensibly between Essex and his brother Anthony—exhibiting the loyalty and love of the former for the Queen. The letters were composed by Bacon, and while they are interesting as specimens of the author's literary power, and are illustrative of his "chameleonlike instinct of adapting his style to his atmosphere," they were calculated, by the interpolation of artful passages, to advance the interests of Bacon, rather than those of Essex, with the Queen. It is significant also that the demeanour which Bacon in these letters caused the Earl to assume, he used against him when Essex was subsequently arraigned for treason. Unless we are prepared to accept the statements of Bacon in this connection, it is impossible to view his participation in this second trial without a feeling of the deepest abhorrence. Bacon had no right to be in Court at all. As one of the "learned counsel," his presence was not required, but in the capacity of "friend of the accused," his evidence could not fail to be greatly damaging to the Earl's case. He proffered his evidence, not only with readiness, but with a ferocious efficacy. We have no evidence beyond Bacon's own word—the word of a man who was striving to put the best complexion on a foul act of treachery—that he deprecated the task. "Skilfully confusing together" the original proposal, and the abortive execution of Essex's outbreak, he insisted that the rising, which in truth was a sudden after-thought, was the result of three months' deliberation, and he concentrated all his efforts on proving that Essex was "not only a traitor, but a hypocritical traitor." No other piece of evidence adduced at the trial had greater weight in procuring the verdict against the Earl. Bacon subsequently pleaded in extenuation of his behaviour that he was acting under pressure from the Crown, but we have the knowledge that on the first occasion he had offered his services, and we can only conclude that at the price of sacrificing the friend who had loaded him with kindnesses, he had determined to make this trial a stepping-stone to Royal favour. To serve this end, friendship, honour, obligation were brushed aside; for, as Bacon has said in one of his essays, the man who wishes to succeed "must know all the conditions of the serpent." The price Bacon received for the blood of Essex was £1,200, or £6,000 in our currency. "The Queen," he wrote to a friendly creditor, "hath done somewhat for me, though not in the perfection I hoped." Bacon had, it is fair to infer from this remark, betrayed his friend; had, in fact, delivered him to the headsman for the hope of pecuniary reward.

FRANCIS BACON AS LORD CHANCELLOR (VANSOMER)
Fr. verulam Cano

BACON, THE FRIEND OF ESSEX AND CECIL.

In what degree Bacon was responsible for the drawing up of a *Declaration of the Treasons of Essex*, which Lord Clarendon described as a "pestilent libel," is impossible to decide. He tells us that his task was little more than that of an amanuensis to the Council and the Queen, but this excuse fails him in the case of his *Apology*, put forth as a vindication of the author in the estimation of the nobles, from the charge of having been false to the Earl of Essex. The paper is admittedly full of inaccuracies, conveying to us the picture, "not of his actual conduct, but of what he felt his conduct ought to have been." Dr. Abbott dismisses this literary and historical effort as interesting only as a "psychological history of the manifold and labyrinthine self-deception to which great men have been subjected."

On the accession of James I., Bacon again threw himself into the political arena, determined to neglect no chance of ingratiating himself with the new Sovereign. He poured forth letters to any and everybody who had the power to forward his cause. He dwelt in these epistles upon the services of his brother Anthony, who had carried on secret and intimate negotiations with Scotland. Sir Thomas Challoner, the confirmed friend of Essex, received a letter from him; he appealed to the Earl of Northumberland; and became the "humble and much devoted" servant of Lord Southampton, on the eve of that nobleman's release from the Tower (where Bacon had helped to place him as an accomplice of Essex). To each he turned with the same request that they would bury the axe, and "further his Majesty's good conceit and inclination towards me."

At this time, Bacon, desperately apprehensive of rebuff, was anxious to conciliate all parties, and to secure friends at Court. He was willing, nay, eager, to be Greek, Roman, or Hebrew, in order to attain his object—even he would avow a gift of poesy to make his calling and election sure. Writing to Sir John Davies, the poet, Bacon, the politician and philosopher, who did not publish two lines of rhyme until twenty-one years later, desired him to "be good to concealed poets." Reading this statement in connection with the other epistles he indicted at the same crisis, we realise how little dependence can be placed upon the implied confession that he had written anonymous poetry. His letters to Southampton, to Michael Hickes (Cecil's confidential man), to David Foules and Sir Thomas Challoner, and to the King himself, all betray the same feverish desire to be all things to all men. He assured Hickes that Lord Cecil is "the person in the State" whom he "loves most," and at the same moment he placed his whole services at the disposal of Cecil's rival, the Earl of Northumberland! When the star of Northumberland began to pale, Bacon importuned Cecil to procure him a knighthood to gratify the ambition of an "Alderman's daughter, a handsome maiden," whom he had found "to my liking." But for a while Bacon found the struggle for recognition unavailing. The King found him an acquired taste—or rather a taste that his Majesty had yet to acquire—and after grovelling to all and sundry, he desisted at the moment from the attempt to gain the King's grace, "because he had completely failed, and for no other reason."

But although Bacon went into retirement, he divided his leisure between his literary labours and his quest for political advancement. In all his political pamphlets, his one ambition was to divine and reflect the Royal views. In 1590 he had nothing but condemnation for the Nonconformist party; in 1604 he had strenuously pleaded the cause of Nonconformity; in 1616 he as strenuously opposed the slightest concession being made to the Nonconformers. In 1604 he was returned to Parliament; three years later, his zeal in anticipating the King's wishes, and supporting his proposals, was rewarded by his appointment to the Solicitor-Generalship. In the following year he was made clerk of the Star Chamber, and immediately set himself to secure the displacement of Hobart, the Attorney-General.

Bacon's conduct towards the Earl of Essex has already been considered. Had this been the only instance of the kind in his career, his apologists would have achieved something more than public opinion can grant them in their endeavours to explain it away. But his behaviour towards Cecil is another lurid illustration of his duplicity and ingratitude. During the last fourteen years of his life Cecil had been the friend and patron of Bacon, whose letters to him are couched in almost passionate terms of loyalty and "entire devotion." In one epistle he declares himself "empty of matter," but "out of the fulness of my love," he writes to express "my continual and incessant love for you, thirsting for your return." Cecil was his refuge and deliverer in 1598, and again in 1603, when he was arrested for debt, and Bacon was not empty of reason when he asserted in another letter, "I write to myself in regard to my love to you, you being as near to me in heart's blood as in blood of descent." In 1611, a short while before Cecil's death, he wrote this last profession of his affection:—

"I do protest before God, without compliment, that if I knew in what course of life to do you best service, I would take it, and make my thoughts, which now fly to many pieces, be reduced to that centre."

In May of 1612 Cecil died. Within a week Bacon had proffered his services to the King in the place of his cousin, of whom he wrote:—

"He (Cecil) was a fit man to keep things from growing worse, but no very fit man to reduce things to be much better; for he loved to keep the eyes of all Israel a little too much upon himself."

To another, he wrote that Cecil "had a good method, if his means had been upright," and again to the King, on the same subject:—

"To have your wants, and necessities in particular, as it were hanged up in two tablets before the eyes of your Lords and Commons, to be talked of for four months together; to stir a number of projects and then blast them, and leave your Majesty nothing but the scandal of them; to pretend even carriage between your Majesty's rights and the ease of the people, and to satisfy neither—these courses, and others the like, I hope, are gone with the deviser of them."

Less than a year before, Bacon had protested before God, "without compliment," his desire to serve Cecil, and now he protests to God in this letter to the King, that when he noted "your zeal to deliver the Majesty of God from the vain and indign comprehension of heresy and degenerate philosophy ... *perculsit ilico animum* that God would shortly set upon you some visible favour; and let me not live if I thought not of the taking away of that man"—the man as "near to me in heart's blood as in the blood of descent."

FRANCIS BACON AS LORD CHANCELLOR

The Right Honble Francis Bacon, Baron Verulam and Viscount St Albans, Lord High Chancellor of England.

The King, who had grown weary of Cecil, may have accepted his death as a visible favour of God, but the favour did not evidently embrace the substitution of Bacon in his cousin's stead. His application for the vacant post of Lord Treasurer was passed over by the King, but Bacon became Attorney-General in the following year.

BACON AS THE CREATURE OF BUCKINGHAM.

Let us regard another trait in the character of this many-sided statesman. To relieve the King's pressing necessities it was proposed that voluntary contributions should be made by the well-affected. The contributions, commonly known as Benevolences, were rarely voluntary; the "moral pressure" that was employed in their collection made them in reality extortions, and, as such, they were the cause of national dissatisfaction. During the search of the house of a clergyman named Peacham, consequent on some ecclesiastical charge, a sermon was found predicting an uprising of the people against this oppressive tax, and foretelling that the King might die like Ananias or Nabal. The sermon had neither been issued nor uttered, but the unfortunate rector, a very old man, was indicted for conspiracy and, in contravention of the law, put to the torture. Peacham had not been convicted of treason, though Bacon "hopes that the end will be good;" or, in other words, that he will be able to wring from the condemned man a confession to make good the charge.

The wretched old clergyman, after being examined in Bacon's presence, "before torture, in torture, between torture, and after torture," could not be made to convict himself, and Bacon's comment to the King is that the man's "raging devil seemeth to be turned into a dumb devil." It will be noted that this infamous act of illegality and Bacon's commentary are the deed and words of the man who is supposed by some to have declared,

> "The quality of mercy is not strain'd;
> It droppeth as the gentle rain from heaven
> Upon the place beneath; it is twice bless'd;
> It blesseth him that gives, and him that takes;
> 'Tis mightiest in the mightiest; it becomes
> The throned monarch better than his crown."

We have seen Bacon as the ingrate, and Bacon as the brute; let us observe him "the meanest of mankind," as Pope described him—who, as Abbott admits, although he refuses Pope's description, "on sufficient occasion could creep like a very serpent." The sufficient occasion was the sudden advance into fame of George Villiers, afterwards Duke of Buckingham. The disgrace and imprisonment of Robert Carr, Earl of Somerset, whose conviction Bacon laboured so strenuously to accomplish, doubtless inspired the Attorney-General with the hope of becoming the chief adviser of the Sovereign. Great must have been his mortification when he discovered the impregnability of Villiers in the favour of the King. But although cast down, Bacon was not abashed. He had, on a previous occasion of disappointment, declared that "service must creep where it cannot go" (*i.e.*, walk upright), and he at once determined to creep into the King's confidence through the medium of the rising Favourite. Instantly, Bacon was on his knees to the new star. "I am yours," he wrote, with more servile want of restraint than he had disclosed in his letters to Essex or Cecil, "surer to you than to my own life." In speech and behaviour he lived up to his protest. He beslavered Villiers with flattery to his face, and he carolled his praises to those whom he felt assured would repeat his words to the spoiled Favourite. His reward was not long in the coming. In 1617 he was made Lord Keeper. He took his seat in Chancery with the most extravagant pomp, his retinue exceeding all his predecessors, says a correspondent of Carleton, "in the bravery and multitude of his servants." The following day he wrote of the ceremony to Villiers, "There was much ado, and a great deal of the world. But this matter of pomp, which is heaven to some men, is hell to me, or purgatory at least." This expression, if not an affectation entirely, is, at least, strangely inconsistent with the account of the vulgar pomp and display of a *Feast of the Family*, which is described by Bacon with so much detail in *The New Atlantis*.

14 BACON AND SHAKESPEARE

THE MONUMENT OF LORD BACON IN ST. MICHAEL'S CHURCH.

In this year Bacon dared to interpose, for a fitful instant, between Villiers and his desires; the next moment he is reduced to a state of pathetic contrition. But the evanescent display of a spirit of independence nearly cost the Lord Keeper his position at Court. For purely personal reasons Bacon regarded, with aversion, the projected marriage between Sir John Villiers, a brother of Buckingham, and the daughter of his old rival and enemy, Sir Edward Coke. In a letter to the Earl of Buckingham he so far forgot himself and his repeated promises to hold himself as a mere instrument in the hands of the King, as to protest against the proposed marriage. Realising immediately the folly of this want of tact, he wrote to the King, and to Buckingham, justifying, or rather excusing his temerity. The King replied with a sharp rebuke, the Favourite in a short, angry note. Further letters elicited additional curt corrections from the angered Monarch, and from Buckingham. Bacon then, for the first time, realised the enormity of his presumption. His position was in danger. Excuse and justification were unavailing to conciliate his angry masters; absolute submission was the only way out of his predicament. Bacon submitted; he even offered to put his submission into writing to the Favourite. Buckingham, in a pencilled note, couched in tones in which arrogance is mixed with acrimonious reflection on "his confused and childish" presumption, notified his forgiveness. In reply, Bacon protested his gratitude to "my ever best Lord, now better than yourself," and concluded, "it is the line of my life, and not the lines of my letter, that must express my thankfulness; wherein, if I fail, then God fail me, and make me as miserable, as I think myself at this time happy, by this reviver through his Majesty's clemency and your incomparable love and favour."

His submission nullified his early resolve not to tolerate any attempts to interfere with the course of law, and delivered him bodily into the hands of Buckingham. The Favourite took the Lord Keeper at his word, and although he put his loyalty to constant and severe tests, by making frequent application to him in favour of chancery suitors, Bacon never again forgot that "the lines of his life" must progress in undeviating conformity with the Favourite's will. It is not profitable here to attempt to determine whether or not he gave verdicts against his own judgment, but we have the letters to show that he listened, replied, and complied with Buckingham's requests, and in 1618 he was made Lord Chancellor, doubtless by the influence, and on the advice, of the Favourite.

During the period of Bacon's temporary disgrace, "when the King and Buckingham had set their faces against him, and all the courtiers were yelping at his heels," the only friend who remained staunch and constant to him was Sir Henry Yelverton, the Attorney-General. Yelverton, whose admiration for, and loyalty towards the Lord Chancellor were unswerving, would truckle neither to the Favourite nor to the King; although the former had assured him that those who opposed him "should discern what favour he had by the power he would use." Within a year of Bacon's restoration to favour Yelverton came into collision with Buckingham, and the Attorney's accidental misconstruction of the King's verbal instructions, served as an excuse for an information to be laid against him in the Star Chamber. We have seen how Bacon could repay friendship with ingratitude, and kindness with baseness in the case of Essex and of Cecil, but, in the instance of Yelverton, even his admirers are forced to admit that his behaviour was "peculiarly cold-blooded and ungrateful." But the "lines of his life" had made him the serf of the Favourite, and "whatever other resolutions Bacon may have broken, none can accuse him of breaking this." When the case came on, and when "the bill was opened by the King's Sergeant briefly, with tears in his eyes, and Mr. Attorney, standing at the Bar, amid the ordinary Counsellors, with dejected looks, weeping tears, and a brief, eloquent, and humble oration, made a submission, acknowledging his error, but denying the corruption"—the Lord Chancellor did his utmost to resist the merciful proposal of the majority to submit the Attorney's submission to the King. The King declined to interfere, and the termination of the case was announced to Buckingham by Bacon, in the following self-satisfied and congratulatory note:—"Yesterday we made an end of Sir Henry Yelverton's causes. I have almost killed myself with sitting almost eight hours. But I was resolved to sit it through." He then gives the terms of the sentence, and adds: "How I stirred the Court I leave it to others to speak; but things passed to his Majesty's great honour." In other words, a blunt, straightforward, and honourable man, who had refused to purchase his office by bribes, or by flattery, had been condemned, on a charge of corruption (of which his judges knew him to be guiltless), to a fine of £4,000 and imprisonment during the King's pleasure, for the offence of refusing to cringe to Buckingham. These were the things that, in Bacon's judgment, "passed to his Majesty's great honour."

In 1618 Bacon became Baron Verulam of Verulam; three years later he was created Viscount St. Alban, "with all the ceremonies of robes and coronet." But his disgrace and discomfiture were soon to come. "In a few weeks," writes Lord Macaulay, "was signally brought to the test the value of those objects for which Bacon had sullied his integrity, had resigned his independence, had violated the most sacred obligations of friendship and gratitude, had flattered the worthless, had persecuted the innocent, had tampered with judges, had tortured prisoners, had plundered suitors, had wasted on paltry intrigue all the powers of the most exquisitely constructed intellect that has ever been bestowed on any of the children of men." On March the 14th, 1621, Bacon was charged by a disappointed suitor with taking money for the dispatch of his suit. On April the 30th, in the House of Lords, was read "the confession and humble submission of me, the Lord Chancellor." On May the 3rd, the Lords came to a general conclusion that "the Lord Chancellor is guilty of the matters wherewith he is charged," and it was resolved that he should be fined £40,000, imprisoned in the Tower during the King's pleasure, declared incapable of any office, place, or employment in the State or Commonwealth, and that he should never sit in Parliament, nor come within the verge of the Court. Five years later, on April the 9th, 1626, he died at Highgate of a chill and sudden sickness, contracted by exposure when stuffing a fowl with snow to test the effect of snow in preserving flesh from putrefaction. He wrote, on his death bed, to Lord Arundel, to whose house he had been carried: "As for the experiment it succeeded exceeding well."

BACON AS THE CREATURE OF BUCKINGHAM.

SIR NICHOLAS BACON.

From the original of Zucchero, in the collection of His Grace the Duke of Bedford.

BACON AND SHAKESPEARE CONTRASTED.

The argument of the Baconians—the term is uniformly employed here to mean the supporters of the Baconian theory of the authorship of Shakespeare—is based on the honest belief that the varied qualifications necessary for the production of the Plays were possessed by only one man of the period in which they were written. And having resolutely determined that the man could be no other than Francis Bacon, they set themselves to work with the same resoluteness, to bend, twist, and contort all facts and evidence to suit their theory. It is clearly impossible to credit any of Shakespeare's contemporary dramatists with the authorship, because their acknowledged work is so immeasurably inferior to his, that any such suggestion must appear ridiculous. It is safe to assume that no writer who had produced poems or plays inferior to those of Shakespeare could be attributed with the authorship of these plays—Shakespeare can only be compared with himself. And the only author who cannot be compared, in this way, to his instant discomfiture, is Bacon, whose published work is, in form and style and essence utterly dissimilar from that of Shakespeare. If a brilliant intellect, wide knowledge, and classical attainments were the only requisite qualifications for the production of the greatest poetry of the world, then Bacon's claim would stand on a sure foundation. He was intimately acquainted, no man better, with the philosophy of the law; he was an eminent classical scholar, a writer of beautiful English, compact in expression, and rich in fancy. He had an extensive acquaintance with literature and history, he was a brilliant orator; but unto all these great gifts was not added the gentle nature, the broad sympathy and knowledge of humanity, the wealth of humour, the depth of passion, the creative power of poetry, which is so strikingly manifested in the plays of William Shakespeare.

Our knowledge of the gentleness of Shakespeare's nature, his uprightness, his honesty, his modesty, is disclosed in his poems, and corroborated by the evidence of his contemporaries. His poetry breathes the gentleness and the lovable nature with which his personal friends credited him. What is there in any analysis of Bacon, beyond his marvellous mental attainments, which single him out as the probable, even possible, creator of King Lear, Brutus, Juliet, Rosalind, and Shylock? Coldness of heart, and meanness of spirit, are faults of temperament which cannot, by the greatest stretch of imagination be associated with the author of Lear's desolating pathos and Arthur's deeply pathetic appeal to Hubert. The points in Bacon's career, which have been dealt with in the foregoing pages, were selected of *malice prepense*; not to detract from the greatness of the Lord Chancellor, as a literary genius and philosopher, but as demonstrating the impossibility of associating such a nature with the authorship of the poetry attributed to him. By his deeds we know him to have been a man whose nature was largely made up of ingratitude, untruth, flattery, meanness, cruelty, and servility. His treatment of Essex, of Cecil, and of Yelverton, can only be stigmatised as "peculiarly cold-blooded and ungrateful;" his persecution of Peacham convicts him of cruelty, bordering on savageness; his meanness is illustrated by the selfish unreasonableness displayed by his attitude towards Trott, his long-suffering creditor. His servile submission to Buckingham has scarcely a parallel in English history.

Deep as was his mind, and profound his knowledge, Bacon possessed no high standard of virtue or morality; he had no intuitive knowledge of mankind, and even as regards his dealings with the people amongst whom his life was passed, he evidenced a singular defectiveness as a reader of character. The sweeping generalities of his observations would be a poor stock-in-trade for a writer of melodrama. In his books he exhibits the cunning, the casuistry and unscrupulousness of an Elizabethan politician and time server. His advice and his opinions betray a mean view of life and its obligations. He had no sense of duty towards his fellow men where duty clashed with his personal interests. His methods are instinct with craft, artifice, and finesse—his advice to Essex, and to the King, was, for this very reason, misleading and abortive. It is incontrovertible that Bacon's writings and Shakespeare's plays are crammed with all kinds of erudition, and Coleridge has claimed for the latter that they form "an inexhaustible mine of virgin wealth." But not a single argument can be advanced to show that Shakespeare could not easily have acquired such erudition and scholarship as the writing of the plays entailed, while we have all the books of Bacon to prove that the poetic genius, the colossal personality, the deep, intense appreciation of nature, and the unrivalled knowledge of man, which are the sovereign mark of the Plays, were not possessed by Bacon.

In editing the existing biographies of Lord Bacon to bolster up their theory, the Baconians have only conformed to the laws of absolute necessity. The cold, unvarnished facts that have been set forth in the foregoing pages are so contrary to the popular impression of what constitutes a "concealed poet," that a more than ordinary amount of colorisation was required to make them acceptable in the author of *The Tempest*. But although there is reasonable excuse, and even some justification for this rose-colorisation process as applied to Bacon—for great men have almost invariably been given, by their biographers, the greatest benefit that be derived from all doubts—the champions of Bacon have far exceeded their prerogative in their attempts to defame and belittle Shakespeare. So much incorrect deduction, so much groundless suspicion, and so much palpable inaccuracy have been put forward by the Baconians, that it is imperative the few known facts in the poet's life should be clearly stated. The following sketch is frankly intended, not so much to support the claim of Shakespeare as the author of the Plays, as to refute the many misconceptions and untruths by which his enemies have endeavoured to traduce him.

BACONIAN FALLACIES RESPECTING SHAKESPEARE.

It is only necessary to read the facts concerning Shakespeare's ancestry and parentage to dissipate some of the absurd suggestions as to the obscurity and illiteracy of the family. The poet came of good yeoman stock, and his forebears to the fourth and fifth generation were fairly substantial landowners. John Shakespeare, his father, was at one period of his life a prosperous trader in Stratford-on-Avon. He played a prominent part in municipal affairs, and became successively Town Councillor, Alderman, one of the chamberlains of the borough, and auditor of the municipal accounts. The assertion that he could not write is a distinct perversion of fact, as "there is evidence in the Stratford archives that he could write with facility."

On the subject of the education of William Shakespeare it is inevitable that there should be conflicting opinions. Those who would deck out the memory of Bacon with the literary robe, "the garment which," according to Mr. R. M. Theobald, is "too big and costly" for the "small and insignificant personality" of Shakespeare, will not concede that he was better educated than his father, who—the error does not lose for want of repetition—"signed his name by a mark." Supporters of the traditional theory, however, reply, "we do not require evidence to show that he was an educated man—we have his works, and the evidence of Ben Jonson, John Heming, and Henry Condell to prove it." Mr. Theobald argues that because there is no positive proof that he had any school education, it is logical to conclude that he had none. Mr. A. P. Sinnett, with the same reckless disregard for facts, says, "We know that he (William Shakespeare) was the son of a tradesman at Stratford, who could not read or write." And in another place, "there is no rag of evidence that he (William Shakespeare) ever went to school." Mr. W. H. Mallock describes him, still without "a rag of evidence" to support his assertion, as "a notoriously ill-educated actor, who seems to have found some difficulty in signing his own name." All evidence we have to guide us on this point of Shakespeare's schooling is that he was entitled to free tuition at the Grammar School at Stratford, which was re-constituted on a mediæval foundation by Edward VI. As the son of a prominent and prosperous townsman, he would, for a moral certainty, have been sent by his father to school (Mr. Sidney Lee favours the probability that he entered the school in 1571), where he would receive the ordinary instruction of the time in the Latin language and literature. The fact that the French passages in *Henry V.* are grammatically correct, but are not idiomatic, makes it certain that they were written by a school-taught linguist, and not by a man like Bacon, who, from his lengthy residence on the Continent, must have been a master of colloquial, idiomatic French. Ben Jonson, in his profound, and somewhat self-conscious command of classical knowledge, spoke slightingly of Shakespeare's "small Latin and less Greek," which is all that his plays would lead us to credit him with. His liberal use of translations, and his indebtedness to North's translations of *Plutarch's Lives*, also substantiates this theory.

We cannot regard, as a great scholar, an author who "gives Bohemia a coast line, makes Cleopatra play billiards, mixes his Latin, and mulls his Greek." Mr. Reginald Haines, who has made a study of Shakespeare for the express purpose of testing his classical attainments, denies emphatically that he shows any acquaintance with Greek at all. His conclusions are worthy of consideration: "Of course there are common allusions to Greek history and mythology such as every poet would have at command, but no reference at first hand to any Greek writer.... As far as I know there are but four real Greek words to be found in Shakespeare's works—*threne, cacodemon, practic,* and *theoric*. It is impossible to suppose that Bacon could have veiled his classical knowledge so successfully in so extensive a field for its display, or that he could, for instance, have perpetrated such a travesty of Homer as appears in *Troilus and Cressida*. With Latin, the case is somewhat different. Shakespeare certainly knew a little grammar-school Latin. He was familiar with Ovid, and even quotes him in the original; and he certainly knew Virgil, and Seneca, Cæsar, and something of Terence and Horace, and, as I myself believe, of Juvenal. But he very rarely quotes Latin, unless it be a proverb or some stock quotation from Mantuanus or a tag from a Latin grammar. When he uses conversational Latin, as in *Love's Labour's Lost*, the idiom is shaky. The quotations from Horace, &c., in *Titus Andronicus* are certainly not by Shakespeare. Nor are the Latinisms like "palliament" in that play. Still he has a very large vocabulary of Latin words such as *renege,* to *gust* (taste), and we may fairly say that Shakespeare knew Latin as well as many sixth form boys, but not as a scholar." Two years ago a writer in the *Quarterly Review*, who had gone through all the alleged examples of erudition and evidences of wide and accurate classical scholarship in the Shakespearean plays, showed them to be entirely imaginary.

In 1582, before he was nineteen years of age, Shakespeare married Anne Hathaway, and three years afterwards he left Stratford for London. It was during this period, says Mr. Theobald, that "the true Shakespeare was studying diligently, and filling his mind with those vast stores of learning—classic, historic, legal, scientific—which bare such splendid fruit in his after life." As Mr. Theobald's contention is that Bacon was the "true Shakespeare," let us consider for a moment how young Francis was employing his abilities at this particular time. In 1579 he returned to England after a two years' residence in France. He had revealed an early disposition to extend his studies beyond the ordinary limits of literature, and to read the smallest print of the book of nature. He was already importuning his uncle, Lord Burghley, for some advancement which might enable him to dispense with the monotonous routine of legal studies. Failing in this endeavour, he was admitted as a barrister of Gray's Inn, was elected to Parliament for Melcombe Regis, composed his first philosophical work, which he named "with great confidence, and a magnificent title," *The Greatest Birth of Time*, and another treatise entitled, *Advice to Queen Elizabeth*. In the case of the poet we have no record; in that of the future Lord Chancellor we get the key of the nature which rendered the man as "incapable of writing *Hamlet* as of making this planet."

ANNA LADY BACON, MOTHER OF FRANCIS BACON.
(From an original picture in the collection of Lord Verulam at Gorhambury).

William Beeston, a 17th century actor, has left it on record that, after leaving Stratford, Shakespeare was for a time a country schoolmaster. In 1586 he arrived in London. His only friend in the Metropolis was Richard Field, a fellow townsman, whom he sought out, and with whom, as publisher, he was shortly to be associated. It is uncertain when Shakespeare joined the Lord Chamberlain's company of actors, but documentary evidence proves that he was a member of it in 1594, and that in 1603, after the accession of James I., when they were called the King's Players, he was one of its leaders. This company included among its chief members Shakespeare's life-long friends, Richard Burbage, John Heming, Henry Condell, and Augustine Phillips, and it was under their auspices that his plays first saw the light.

Before they opened at the Rose on the Bankside, Southwark, in 1592, the Lord Chamberlain's company had played at The Theatre in Shoreditch, and in 1599 they opened at the Globe, which was afterwards the only theatre with which Shakespeare was professionally associated. In this year he acquired an important share in the profits of the company, and his name appears first on the list of those who took part in the original performance of Ben Jonson's *Every Man in His Humour*. Mr. Theobald states that Shakespeare had become a fairly prosperous theatre manager in 1592, but as he did not secure his interest in the business until seven years later, what probably is meant is that Shakespeare was combining the duties of stage manager, acting manager, and treasurer of the theatre. It would appear that, recognising the fact that the period in Shakespeare's life between 1588 and 1592 is a blank "which no research can fill up," Mr. Theobald considers that he is justified in making good the deficiency out of his own inner consciousness.

As occasion will require that Mr. Theobald's contribution to the controversy shall presently be dealt with, it may not be out of place here to explain the object, so far as it is intelligible, of his *Shakespeare Studies in Baconian Light* (Sampson Low, 1901). It would have been a fair thing to assume that the design of the author of this volume of over 500 pages, was to prove the Baconian authorship of Shakespeare, but as Mr. Theobald has since written to the Press to protest against this interpretation of his motives, we must take his words as he gives his parallels "for what they are worth." In the opening lines of his preface, Mr. Theobald declares that while the greatest name in the world's literature is Shakespeare, there is in the world's literature no greater name than Bacon. Really, it would seem that if his object is not to prove that the two names stand for one and the same individual, this statement is sheer nonsense. Before the end of the preface is reached, he frankly avows his belief that "when the time comes for a general recognition of Bacon as the true Shakespeare, the poetry will still be called "Shakespeare," and that no one will find anything compromising in such language, any more than we do when we refer to George Eliot or George Sand, meaning Miss Evans or Madame Dudevant." But if Mr. Theobald was as versed in his study of the subject as Mrs. Gallup, Dr. Owen, Mr. A. P. Sinnett, or even Bacon himself, he would know that when this general recognition comes to pass the author of the Plays will not be called Shakespeare, or Bacon, but Francis "Tidder, or Tudor"—otherwise Francis I. of England—provided, of course, that the bi-literallists can substantiate their cipher. But as Mr. Theobald does not design to prove the Baconian theory, he does not, of course, require the evidence of the great Chancellor, or he may, as a disparager of cipher speculations, accept such evidence "for what it is worth."

MR. THEOBALD, A BACONIAN BY INTUITION.

Mr. Theobald's "preliminaries" are chiefly remarkable for three diverse reasons. We learn therefrom that he is a Baconian by intuition—"the persuasion took hold of his mind" as soon as Holme's *Authorship of Shakespeare* was placed in his hand—that he does not admit the existence of genius, and that he is intolerant of "clamours and asperities, denunciations and vituperations," and the personal abuse employed by anti-Baconians, whom he alludes to as Hooligans, and compares with geese. So long as he keeps to the trodden path of Baconian argument, he is only about as perverse and incorrect as the rest of—to use his own expression as applied to Shakespearean students—"the clan." But he becomes amusing when he ventures to present new arguments in support of Bacon's claim, variously abusive in his references to Shakespeare, and desperately dogmatic in his pronouncement of the faith that is in him.

"Among the many shallow objections brought against the Baconian theory," writes Mr. Theobald in his chapter on Bacon's literary output, "one is founded on the assumption that Bacon was a voluminous writer, and that if we add to his avowed literary productions, the Shakespearean dramas, he is loaded with such a stupendous literary progeny as no author could possibly generate. Moreover, he was so busy in state business as a lawyer, judge, counsellor, member of Parliament, confidential adviser to the King, and the responsible rulers in State and Church, that he had very little spare time for authorship."

In order to demonstrate that this shallow objection, as Mr. Theobald calls it, is a well-founded and irrefutable statement of fact, we have only to refer to Lord Bacon's life and to his letters. From 1579, when he returned from France, until the end of his life he was distracted between politics and science; he put forward as his reason for seeking office that he might thereby be able to help on his philosophic projects which with him were paramount, and the poignant regret of his last years was that he had allowed himself to be diverted from philosophy into politics. He found "no work so meritorious," so serviceable to mankind, "as the discovery and development of the arts and inventions that tend to civilise the life of men." In his letter to Lord Burghley in 1592, he expressed the hope that in the service of the State he could "bring in industrious observations, grounded conclusions, and profitable inventions and discoveries—the best state of that province"—the province embracing all nature which he had made his own. But office was denied him, and he returned to "business" and to his constant bewailings of the fact that he had no time for literature. In 1607 he settled the plan of the *Instauratio Magna*;

which had been foreshadowed in his *Advancement of Learning*, published two years previously. In 1609 he wrote to Toby Mathew, "My *Instauratio* sleeps not," and again, in the same year, "My great work goeth forward; and after my manner I alter ever when I add; so that nothing is finished till all is finished." From 1609 to 1620 Bacon spent such leisure as he could snatch from his other work in revising the *Novum Organum* (the second part of his *Magna Instauratio*), of which his chaplain, Rawley, says that he had seen "at least twelve copies revised year by year, one after another, and amended in the frame thereof." In 1620, when the *Novum Organum* was published, the author sent it into the world uncompleted, because he had begun to number his days, and "would have it saved." This was the book he alluded to as "my great work"—the work of his life, and he issued it as a fragment because he had not been able to find time to finish it. The belief that he had "very little spare time for authorship" is no shallow objection brought against the Baconian theory—it is an irrefutable fact, proved not only out of the mouth, but in the life, of Lord Bacon.

SIR NATHANIEL BACON.
From the original, in the collection of The Right Hon[ble] the Earl of Verulam.

In spite, however, of all positive evidence to the contrary, Mr. Theobald proceeds to bolster up his contention that Bacon had time, and to spare, for literary pursuits, by the following most amazing piece of logic. He contends, in the first place, that "an estimate of the entire literary output of Bacon, as a scientific and philosophical writer, proves the amount to be really somewhat small." He takes the fourteen volumes of Spedding's *Life and Works*, subtracts the prefaces, notes, editorial comments, and the biographical narrative, puts aside as of "no literary significance whatever," all business letters, speeches, State papers, etc., and thus reduces the total amount of literature to Bacon's credit in the seven volumes devoted to the *Life* to some 375 pages. "If we calculate the whole amount contained in the fourteen volumes, we shall find it may be reckoned at about six such volumes, each containing 520 pages. On this method of calculation and selection, all that Mr. Theobald can find, "for his whole life, amounts to about 70 pages per annum, less than six pages a month." Turning from Bacon to Shakespeare, Mr. Theobald finds that here again is a man whose literary output has been greatly exaggerated, for "if the Shakespeare poetry was the only work of William Shakespeare, certainly he was not a voluminous writer. *Thirty-one years may be taken as a moderate estimate of the duration of his literary life, i.e., from 1585 till his death in 1616.* And the result is 37 plays and the minor poems—not two plays for each year." Mr. Theobald, it will be seen, possesses the same weakness for statistics that Mr. Dick evinced for King Charles' head; he drops in his little estimate in season and out of season, and his appraisements are as manifold as they are fallacious. The period of Shakespeare's dramatic output was confined to twenty years, from 1591 to 1611—if he had continued writing plays till his death in 1616, Bacon's alleged playwriting would not have ceased with such significant suddenness in 1611. But what conclusion does Mr. Theobald arrive at as the result of his estimates? No less than this, that if the whole of Shakespeare, and the whole of Bacon's acknowledged works belong to the same author, "the writer was not a voluminous author—*not by any means so voluminous as Miss Braddon* or Sir Walter Scott." That Mr. Theobald should not hesitate to class Miss Braddon's novels with the plays of Shakespeare, which belong to the supreme rank of literature, or even with Bacon's "royal mastery of language never surpassed, never perhaps equalled," is the most astounding link in this astounding chain of so-called evidence. But Mr. Theobald advances it with the utmost confidence. "Therefore," he sums up, "let this objection stand aside; it vanishes into invisibility as soon as it is accurately tested"—*i.e.*, weighed up, like groceries, by the pound.

Mr. Theobald is scarcely complimentary to Shakespeare's champions in this controversy, but his language is positively libellous when he refers to Shakespeare himself. His personality is "small and insignificant;"—he is a "shrunken, sordid soul, fattening on beer, and coin, and finding sweetness and content in the *stercorarium* of his Stratford homestead"—a "feeble, and funny, and most ridiculous mouse." Mr. Theobald almost argues himself not a Baconian by his assertion that "no Baconian, so far as I know, seeks to help his cause by personal abuse, or intolerant and wrathful speech."

WAS SHAKESPEARE THE "UPSTART CROW?"

ALL that we can allege with any certainty about Shakespeare, between 1586 and 1602, is that he must have obtained employment at one or other of the only two theatres existing in London at that time (The Theatre, and The Curtain)—perhaps, as Malone has recorded, in the capacity of call-boy—that he became an actor, was employed in polishing up the stock-plays presented by the Company, and that *Love's Labour's Lost* was produced in the Spring of 1591. Assuming that Shakespeare was the author of this play—assuming, that is to say, that Ben Jonson, John Heming, and Henry Condell were neither arrant fools, nor wilful perjurers—it is evident that the "insignificant," "shrunken, sordid soul," "this ridiculous mouse" had education, application, a natural taste for the stage; and what is more—and more than Mr. Theobald can comprehend—he had genius. Mr. Theobald does not arrive at any such conclusion. Apart altogether from Mrs. Gallup's cipher revelations, he is convinced by another "flash of intuition" that Ben Jonson was a fellow conspirator with Bacon in the ridiculous plot of foisting Bacon's plays upon the world as the work of Shakespeare, and that Heming and Condell were but the tools of the disgraced Lord Chancellor.

But if Shakespeare was not advancing towards prosperity by the feasible methods I have conjectured, how can Mr. Theobald account for his ultimately emerging from the "depths of poverty" into a position of comparative affluence? The explanation is simplicity itself: "If a needy, and probably deserving vagabond" (page 11).—Why deserving? He was a "shrunken, sordid soul" on page 7!—"dives into the abyss of London life, lies *perdu* for a few years, and then emerges as a tolerably wealthy theatrical manager; you know that he must have gained some mastery of theatrical business." So far the inference is legitimate and convincing; but how? Must he not have disclosed exceptional ability as an actor or playwright, or—? listen to Mr. Theobald!—"he must have made himself a useful man in the green room, a skilful organiser of players and stage effects—he must have found out how to govern a troop of actors, reconciling their rival egotisms, and utilising their special gifts; how to cater for a capricious public, and provide attractive entertainments. Anyhow, he would have little time for other pursuits—if a student at all, his studies would be very practical relating to matters of present or passing interest. *During this dark period he has been carving his own fortune, filling his pockets, not his mind; working for the present, not for the future. But it was exactly then that the plays began to appear.*"

Mr. Theobald's argument can only be described as a reckless, illogical, and absurd distortion of possibilities, and it is the more inconsequential since it proceeds to defeat its primary object. In the first place it is supremely ridiculous to assume that the paltry services of Shakespeare in the green room and the carpenter's shop, secured for him his pecuniary interest in the Globe Theatre, or the respect and friendship of the leading dramatists of his day, or even the enmity of jealous rivals in the craft. Yet Mr. Theobald attempts to substantiate his conclusions by distorting the obvious meaning of Robt. Greene's reference to Shakespeare in *A Groat's Worth of Wit.* Greene was not an actor, but a dramatist; he was a man of dissolute habits, a poet of rare charm, but a playwright of only moderate ability and repute. He was a gentleman by birth, and a scholar by training. He had the lowest opinion of actors—he envied them their success, and despised their avocation. In *The Return from Parnassus* he betrays his prejudice in the following lines, which are put into the mouth of a poor and envious student:—

> "England affords these glorious vagabonds,
> That carried erst their fardels on their backs,
> Coursers to ride on through the gazing streets,
> Sweeping it in their glaring satin suits,
> And pages to attend their masterships;
> With mouthing words that better wits had framed,
> They purchase lands, and now esquires are made."

To the jaundiced mind of Robert Greene, the accumulation of means by an actor was a crime in itself, but that a mere mummer should dare to compete with the scholar and the poet in the composition of plays—more, that he should write plays that exceeded in popularity those of the superior person, the student—was a personal affront. On his death-bed, in 1592, Greene found an outlet for his resentment in writing an ill-natured farewell to life, in which he girded bitterly at the new dramatist, whose early plays had already brought him into public notice. He warns his three brother playwrights—Marlowe, Nash, and Peele—against the "upstart crow, the only Shake-scene in the country" who "supposes he is as well able to bumbast out a blanke verse as the best of you." How it is possible to interpret these words to mean that the "upstart crow" was not an author, "but only an actor who pretended to be an author also," the oldest inhabitant of Colney Hatch and Mr. Theobald must decide between them. These anything but "cryptic" words, as Mr. Theobald describes them, can have but one interpretation, and that is the one their author intended. They do not imply that Shakespeare, the "upstart crow," is not the author of the plays imputed to him, but that he considers his plays as good as those of the older dramatists. His profession of authorship is not questioned, but the quality of his work is savagely challenged. Any other construction put upon the passage is sheer nonsense. Mr. Theobald appeals to the "most gentle and gentlemanly critics" to be patient and tolerant with the Baconians—"men as sound in judgment and as well equipped in learning as yourselves"—but it is high time that this kind of wilful misrepresentation and perversion of common sense should be condemned in plain language. If Greene had believed that Shakespeare was wearing feathers that did not rightfully belong to him, if he were pretending to be what he really was not; if, in Mr. Theobald's confident explanation, he had no right to profess himself an author at all, we may be quite certain that Greene would have said so outright—he would not have adopted a "cryptic" style, and left it for Mr. Theobald to decipher his meaning.

Mr. Theobald's alternative theory that the word "Shake-scene" does not refer to Shakespeare at all, is even more preposterous. "In 1592 'Shakespeare' did not exist at all, and only two or three of the plays which subsequently appeared under this name could have been written." But those two or three plays included, as far as we can tell, *Love's Labour's Lost*, *Two Gentlemen of Verona*, and *The Comedy of Errors*—plays of sufficient promise to secure any author recognition as a poet and dramatist. If Mr. Theobald entertains any serious doubts as to the identification of Shakespeare in the "Shake-scene" of Greene, he may be advised to read the apology for this attack which Henry Chettle, the publisher, prefixed to a tract of Greene's in the same year. "I am as sorry," Chettle wrote, "as if the originall fault had been my fault, because myselfe have seene his (*i.e.*, Shakespeare's) demeanour no lesse civill than he (is) exelent in the qualitie he professes, besides divers of worship have reported his uprightness of dealing, which argues his honesty and his facetious grace in writing that aprooves his art."

ST. MICHAEL'S CHURCH.
Extract from the Will of Lord Bacon.

"For my burial I desire it may be in St. Michael's Church, near St. Albans; there was my Mother buried, and it is the only Christian Church within the walls of Old Verulam.

"For my name and memory I leave it to men's charitable speeches, and to foreign nations, and the next ages."

This apology put forth by Henry Chettle is an invaluable attestation to the character and literary standing of Shakespeare—"his uprightness in dealing" is a matter of public report, and "his facetious grace in writing" is frankly acknowledged. At a period when professional rivalries ran strong, and no man's reputation was above attack, a publisher and fellow author is seen regarding Shakespeare not only as a man to whom an apology was due, but to whom it appeared expedient to make one. In treating of the personal history of Shakespeare, it must be borne in mind that although the duly-attested facts regarding him are regrettably few, the poet was widely known to the leading literary and theatrical men of his day. Ben Jonson, his brother actor and dramatist, and Michael Drayton were his intimate friends. Condell and Heming remained in close relationship with Shakespeare until his death, and Richard Burbage was his partner in the business of the Globe Theatre. In *Pericles* and *Timon*, Shakespeare worked in collaboration with George Wilkins, a dramatic writer of some repute, and William Rowley, a professional reviser of plays. There were besides, the members of the Globe Company, men who lived their lives beside him, rehearsed under him, learned from him, interpreted him. Yet none of these men appear to have entertained the slightest doubt upon the genuineness of his claims to authorship, while every contemporaneous reference to him is couched in terms of affection and admiration. The only possible explanation of this remarkable fact is that Shakespeare and Bacon were one and the same person—a theory that the most hardened Baconian has not yet thought it advisable to advance.

WM. SHAKESPEARE, MONEY LENDER AND POET.

MR. Theobald is unfortunate in his selection of the points he raises in Shakespeare's career in order to belittle the character of the poet. He writes: "His known occupations, apart from theatre business, were money-lending, malt-dealing, transactions in house and land property." There is not the slightest evidence to show that Shakespeare traded as a money-lender; his only interest in malt-dealing was confined to one transaction, and his transactions in houses and lands were those of any man who invests his savings in real estate. The phrase is, as the most superficial Shakespeare student will recognise, misleading in substance, and incorrect as a statement of fact. In another part of his determinedly one-sided book, Mr. Theobald dismisses, in a paragraph, the contention that Shakespeare's poems are illuminated and illustrated by Shakespeare's life. The obvious rejoinder is that there is nothing in the life of Shakespeare that makes it difficult for us to accept him as the author of the Plays, whereas the whole life and character of Bacon makes his pretensions more than difficult, even impossible, of acceptance.

In 1593, *Venus and Adonis* was published by Shakespeare's friend and fellow townsman, Richard Field, and in the following year *Lucrece* was issued at the sign of the White Greyhound in St. Paul's Churchyard. Both poems were dedicated to Shakespeare's first and only patron, the Earl of Southampton, with whom Bacon is not known to have sought any intimacy until 1603, when he addressed to him a characteristic letter of conciliation. (In 1621, when Bacon was accused of corruption, the Earl of Southampton pointed out the insufficiency of the Lord Chancellor's original confession, and it was largely the result of his firm and unfriendly attitude that Bacon's abject submission and acknowledgment of the justice of the charges, was placed before the Lords). These poems constituted Shakespeare's appeal to the reading public. The response was instantaneous and enthusiastic. "Critics vied with each other," writes Mr. Sidney Lee, "in the exuberance of the eulogies, in which they proclaimed that the fortunate author had gained a place in permanence on the summit of Parnassus." *Lucrece*, Michael Drayton declared, in his *Legend of Matilda* (1594), was "revived to live another age." In 1595, William Clerke, in his *Polimanteia*, gave "all praise" to "Sweet Shakespeare" for his *Lucrecia*. John Weever, in a sonnet addressed to "honey-tongued" Shakespeare in his *Epigrams* (1595), eulogised the two poems as an unmatchable achievement, although he mentions the plays *Romeo*, and *Richard*, and "more whose names I know not." Richard Carew, at the same time, classed him with Marlowe, as deserving the praises of an English Catullus. Printers and publishers of the poems strained their resources to satisfy the demands of eager purchasers. No fewer than seven editions of *Venus* appeared between 1594 and 1602; an eighth followed in 1617. *Lucrece* achieved a fifth edition in the year of Shakespeare's death. The Queen quickly showed him special favour, and until her death in 1603, Shakespeare's plays were repeatedly acted in her presence.

ELIZABETH R

When the sonneteering vogue reached England from Italy and France, Shakespeare applied himself to the composition of sonnets, with all the force of his poetic genius. Of the hundred and fifty-four sonnets that survive, the greater number were probably composed in 1593 and 1594. Many are so burdened with conceits and artificial quibbles that their literary value is scarcely discernible; but the majority, on the other hand, attain to supreme heights of poetic expression, sweetness, and imagery. They are of peculiar interest, as disclosing the relationship that existed between Southampton and Shakespeare. No less than twenty of the sonnets are undisguisedly addressed to the patron of the poet's verse: three of them are poetical transcriptions of the devotion which he expressed to Southampton in his dedicatory preface to *Lucrece*. The references are direct and unmistakable. In 1603, when the accession of James I. opened the gates of Southampton's prison, Bacon was meekly writing to him: "I would have been very glad to have presented my humble service to your Lordship by my attendance if I could have foreseen that it should not have been unpleasing to you," and hypocritically assuring him, "How credible soever it may seem to you at first, yet it is as true as a thing God knoweth, that this great change (*i.e.*, the release of Southampton, and his favour with the new monarch, whose good-will Bacon ardently desired), hath wrought in me no other change towards your Lordship than this, that I may safely be now that which I was truly before." The Earl of Southampton considered these protestations of friendship so incredible, as coming from the man who had consigned Essex, Bacon's own friend and patron, to the headsman, and sent Southampton himself to the Tower, that he appears to have made no response to this letter, and twenty years afterwards he materially contributed to the Lord Chancellor's discomfiture. One has only to compare this letter with the sonnet with which Shakespeare saluted his patron on his release from the Tower, to recognise the impossibility of regarding the two compositions as the work of the same man.

THE "TRUE SHAKESPEARE."

If Bacon was the "true Shakespeare," as Mr. Theobald calls him, the question naturally arises as to his motive in concealing the authorship of the plays and the poems. Baconians explain this extraordinary act of reticence on the ground that dramatic authorship was held in low esteem, and that the fact, if known, would have proved an obstacle to his advancement at Court. This contention, though fully borne out by Bacon's cipher writings, is ridiculous in the extreme. In the first place, it was not the profession of dramatic authorship, but the calling of the actor that was held in low esteem. Furthermore, poetry was not under the ban that attached to the stage, and it cannot be denied that the acknowledged authorship of *Venus and Adonis*, of *Lucrece*, or of the *Sonnets*, would have won for Bacon more favour at Elizabeth's Court than he ever secured by his philosophy. Poetry was held in high esteem; sonneteering was the vogue. Buckingham, in the next reign, wrote a play, *The Rehearsal*, and Essex had composed a masque. The publication of *The Faerie Queene*, in 1589, secured for Edmund Spenser an introduction to the Queen, who made him her poet laureate in the same year. Why should Bacon have persisted in devoting himself to a branch of literature which appears to have advanced his interests so little? Elizabeth was never impressed by his genius; she acknowledged his great wit and learning, but accounted him "not deep." James criticised his philosophy with lofty captiousness, and compared his *Novum Organum* to "the peace of God, which passeth all understanding." It would be neither discreditable to his pride as a poet, nor contrary to the nature of the man, to believe that if he could safely have claimed the authorship of *Lucrece* and *A Midsummer Night's Dream*, he would not have hesitated for an hour in so doing. *Venus and Adonis* won for Shakespeare the favour of Elizabeth, while, under the sovereignty of her successor, Shakespeare's company gave between forty and fifty performances at Court during the first five years of his reign. Is it not rather absurd to believe that Bacon should have remained quiescent while his unavowed work was being acclaimed as "immortal," and the works published under his own name were either neglected, or treated to a contemptuous *mot* by the very person whose admiration he was feverishly striving to attract?

Yet the Baconians find no difficulty in accepting this explanation of secrecy — Mr. A. P. Sinnett regards the motive as perfectly intelligible. Bacon, he contends, was not writing his plays for fame, but for the money it brought him. Mr. Theobald contends that the plays could not have been written by Shakespeare because he was too busily employed in "carving his own fortune" ... "filling his pockets" ... "working for the present, not for the future," to devote the necessary leisure to literary pursuits. Bacon himself, according to the bi-literal cipher discoveries of Mrs.

Gallup, declares that so far from receiving remuneration for his plays, he paid "a sufficient reward in gold" to Shakespeare for the use of his name. "He was left quite without resources," Mr. Sinnett explains, "and he took up dramatic writing for the sake of the money it earned him." Before we are won over by this fallacious explanation, we would inquire how it was that Bacon, who was left without resources in 1577, did not produce his first play until 1591, and then paid for the luxury of concealing his indiscretion. Mr. Sinnett's next sentence is instructive as a specimen of Baconian reasoning. "After Bacon obtained an office of profit at forty-six, no more Shakespeare plays appeared, though the reputed author lived for ten more years in dignified leisure at Stratford." It may, of course, be regarded as a "shallow objection" to raise, but Bacon was fifty-one years of age when Shakespeare retired to Stratford. Moreover, Bacon obtained no office of profit in 1611. He was made Solicitor-General, and became a rich man, in 1607, but until his appointment to the Attorney-Generalship in 1613 he was continually suing for promotion and applying for a better paid office. It is, indeed, significant that Bacon was silent as a playwright from the time of Shakespeare's retirement. When he was Chancellor, and enjoyed a yearly income equal to between £60,000 and £70,000 of our money, he continued to compose his scientific works, and he was still actively engaged in the task between 1621 and 1626 when he was again reduced to comparative penury, and the more remunerative employment of play-writing would have relieved his financial position without detriment to his political prospects. The source from whence he could have augmented his inadequate income was neglected while he employed himself in writing a *Digest of the Laws of England*, *The History of Henry VII.*, *Sylva Sylvarum*, *Augmentis Scientiarum*, *The Dialogue of the Holy War*, some additional *Essays*, and the translation of "certain Psalms into English verse." Bacon, according to Baconians, produced his plays during the busiest period of his political career, and in the days of his leisure and impecuniosity — "when Shakespeare was not present to shield him from the disgrace of possessing poetic and dramatic genius" — he produced his versification of the Psalms.

ROBERT DEVEREUX, EARL OF ESSEX. O.B. 1601.
From the original of Hilliard, in the collection of The Right Honble the Earl of Verulam.

Mr. Sinnett, in common with Mr. Theobald and, indeed, all other upholders of the Baconian theory, has a distinctly original way of dealing with matters of fact. Mr. Theobald invents his facts to suit his argument; Mr. Sinnett ignores all facts that prove intractable. Thus Mr. Sinnett in *The National Review*: "All through the plays there is no allusion to Stratford." And again: "While Bacon seems to have gone North to curry favour with James on his accession, *Macbeth* was written just after that event. Certainly there is no reason to suppose that Shakespeare ever went to Scotland." What nonsense is all this! Although personalities are rare in the Plays, there are a number of literal references to Stratford, and Shakespeare's native county, in *The Taming of the Shrew*; and local allusions are also to be found in the second part of *Henry IV.* and *The Merry Wives of Windsor*. In his *Life of William Shakespeare*, Mr. Lee enumerates several instances in point. "Barton Heath," we read is, "Barton-on-the-Heath, the home of Shakespeare's aunt, Edmund Lambert's wife, and of her sons. The tinker, in *The Taming of the Shrew*, confesses that he has run up a score with Marian Hacket, the fat ale wife of Wincot. The references to Wincot and the Hackets are singularly precise. The name of the maid of the inn is given as Cicely Hacket, and the ale-house is described in the stage direction as 'on a heath.'" Again, in *Henry IV.*, the local reference to William Visor, of Woncot, and the allusions to the region of the Cotswold Hills, and the peculiar Cotswold custom of sowing "red lammas" wheat at an unusually early season of the agricultural year, are unmistakable. Mr. Sinnett's assumptions that Bacon went to Scotland and that Shakespeare did not, are entirely arbitrary. In point of fact we may be quite sure that Bacon did not go to Scotland, and we have no reason to believe that Shakespeare was ever in Venice, or Sardis, or "a wood near Athens." The author of the *Letters from Hell* was not under suspicion because he could not claim to have been ferried across the Styx to get his local colour.

If we are to accept the Baconian opinion of Shakespeare it is difficult to understand how Bacon came to allow him to make a successful application on behalf of his father, John Shakespeare, to the College of Heralds for a grant of arms in 1597. Bacon was an aristocrat and a firm believer in his order. If he knew Shakespeare to be a notoriously ill-educated actor, a man little better than a vagabond, an impostor, a villain with "some humour," whom Bacon employed as the original model for Sir John Falstaffe and Sir Toe-be—as Mr. Harold Bayley states—why did he not prevent his intimate friend, the Earl of Essex, the Earl of Southampton, and William Camden, the great scholar and antiquary, from being hoaxed by this impudent rogue, and prevent the Shakespeares from obtaining the desired grant? These three friends of Shakespeare certainly facilitated the proceedings.

MR. THEOBALD'S PARALLELS AND MR. BAYLEY'S CONCLUSIONS.

When Mr. Theobald gets away from his biographical pabulum and plunges into the literary arguments for Bacon's authorship of the plays, he has little that is original to reveal, but much that is new in the way of parallels and coincidences. In the first place, he takes it for granted that Shakespeare could not, by any possibility, have written the plays. He does not prove it, but—*cela va sans dire.* Then he proceeds, to the extent of some four hundred pages of matter, to demonstrate, by reference to the significant Baconian characteristics in the plays, and the still more significant parallels between the poetry of Shakespeare and the philosophy of Bacon, that Bacon must be the author of both. Bacon, for instance, appears to have had a "very curious habit" of striking himself on the breast when he wished to emphasise an argument. Brutus, Ophelia, Clarence's little boy, and Claudio, are all represented as using a similar gesture. Some such lamentations as Bacon may be supposed to have uttered after his fall, are to be found in *King Lear,* and Lucrece's self-condemnation of herself to death for an offence of which she is entirely innocent is, of course, inspired by Bacon's behaviour in making a full and humble submission to the Lords in respect of offences which he never committed. The mere fact that *Lucrece* was published in 1594, and that Bacon's downfall did not take place until 1621, is a point of no moment—we can readily agree with Mr. Theobald that "there is a very curious reflection of Bacon's character and temperament in the poem of *Lucrece.*" Lucrece absolves herself in the reflection,

> "The poison'd fountain clears itself again,
> And why not I from this compelled stain?"

Everybody knows that Bacon, "for some time after his condemnation, expected to resume his ordinary functions as counsellor to Parliament, and adviser to the King"—*ergo* Lucrece was Bacon's prototype—in petticoats. Moreover, in the *Essays,* Bacon affixes to a meditative reflection in one of his philosophical propositions the phrase, "I cannot tell." The same phrase, scarcely remarkable in itself, occurs several times in the Plays. Mr. Theobald devotes a whole chapter of his book to emphasising this remarkable coincidence. He advances pages of historical parallels, and he remarks, almost enthusiastically, that both Shakespeare and Bacon have dilated with pitiless logic on "the uselessness of hope."

But Mr. Theobald is most amusing when he compares Bacon's *Essay of Love* with the treatment of Love in Shakespeare. We know Bacon's opinion of love, as expressed in the *Essay,* and we find it difficult to reconcile it with the rhapsodies that we find in the Plays; we remember *Romeo and Juliet,* and the exquisite comment, "Imagine Juliet as the party, loved"—or, rather, we should do so, if Mr. Theobald was not at our elbow to explain the apparent contradiction in thought and term. Love, it would appear, has two sides.

ROBERT DUDLEY, EARL OF LEICESTER.
From an original painting in the possession of The Marquis of Salisbury.

There is the "bosom" side, and the business side. Here we have a full and convincing explanation of the difference between the views of love as expressed in the *Essay*, and the Shakespearean application of the sentiment as displayed in his dramas. In the Plays, Bacon regarded love from the "bosom" point of view, while in the *Essay*, the "very brief, very aphoristic, very concentrated, never discoursive or rhetorical, but severely reflective and practical essay," he was dealing with Juliet as a "business" detail—a contracting party, in short—"the party loved." Nothing could be more convincing! It would almost lead us to entertain a greater admiration for Bacon than Spedding could hope for. He has not only voiced two such entirely contradictory views of love as we find in the *Essay* of Bacon and the plays of Shakespeare, but he has, with the aid of Mr. Theobald, showed that, "curiously enough," the two conflicting expressions are "significantly identical." There is surely no need to proceed further. Mr. Theobald has proved his contention, and we must perforce accept his conclusions that Shakespeare, the arch-impostor, the champion literary fraud of all time, was "either entirely uneducated, or very imperfectly educated; that his Latin was small, his Greek less, and his pure English least of all; that such handwriting as his could never have figured on a University examination paper—this is the opinion, it will be observed, of an M.A., and a former editor of *The Bacon Journal*—that his whole life was too full of business, too much devoted to money to leave any extensive opportunities for study, or for large, broad, world-covering experience."

But if we make it a *sine quâ non* that the writer of the Plays was a man of leisure not devoted to mammon, "with ample opportunity for study, and of a broad-world covering experience" (whatever that may precisely mean), it is proof positive that he was not the man whom we know as Francis Bacon. Bacon's whole life was devoted to business, and to the getting of money; he had no leisure, as he is for ever telling us, for his life's work, and his experience of the world of men was so superficial and misleading that it sent Essex to the block, brought the King to loggerheads with his Parliament, and encompassed the utter downfall and disgrace of the cunning Chancellor. We need not be flustered by Mr. Theobald's hysterical opinion that Shakespeare's writing was "so execrably bad, so unmistakably rustic and plebean, that one may reasonably doubt whether his penmanship extended beyond the capacity of signing his name to a business document," because we have Spedding's statement that Shakespeare's signature is simply characteristic of the caligraphy of the time, and we know by comparison that it is in advance, both in style and legibility, of that of Sir Nicholas Bacon, the father of the great Pretender.

Mr. Harold Bayley, the author of *The Tragedy of Sir Francis Bacon*, is, in the same degree, disdainful of facts. He declares that he will quote verbatim from Mr. Sidney Lee's well-known *Life of Shakespeare* which would be most commendable in him if he did it—but he doesn't. Rather he quotes the opinion of Richard Grant White, who says that "Shakespeare was the son of a Warwickshire peasant," who "signed his name with a mark," and that the Poet was "apprenticed to a butcher." It is but waste of space to repeat that such assertions are palpably false. It may be true, as Mr. Bayley states, that Stratford, in 1595, was in an unsanitary condition, and that the Metropolitan theatres were the resort of undesirable persons—even that Shakespeare entered the play-house as a servitor, but all this proves nothing. It is also true that, up to the time that Shakespeare's plays began to be produced, "there had been nothing in his career that would cause us to suppose he was a sublime genius," but until Homer, or Michael Angelo, or Rudyard Kipling began to produce their masterpieces, we knew of nothing in them to make us accept them as heaven-born geniuses. Mr. Bayley assumes that Shakespeare left Stratford-upon-Avon in 1585 with "*Venus and Adonis, Lucrece*, and, perhaps, *Hamlet*, in his pocket." The reason for his assumption is not vouchsafed to us. True, our dramatist left

Stratford in 1585, but *Venus* was not published until 1593, and it was not until 1602 that *Hamlet* was produced. The mere fact that "in the sixteenth century the provincial dialects were so marked that the county gentry ... had difficulty in making themselves understood, except to their provincial neighbours," proves that both these works were composed after Shakespeare had been for some time a resident in London, and indeed it is ridiculous to suppose that it took him eight years to find a publisher for *Venus and Adonis*. Donnelly deciphered the Bishop of Worcester's opinion that Shakespeare was "a butcher's rude and vulgar apprentice," who "in our opinion was not likely to have writ them (the Plays)." "In our opinion" is scarcely evidence. Mr. Bayley's contemptuous reference to Shakespeare's handwriting as "five strange scrawls," is combated by Spedding's authoritative dictum, and his immediately succeeding conclusion that the classical allusions and references in the Plays prove the author to have been "a cultured aristocrat," robs his entire argument of sapiency or merit.

Mr. Harold Bayley's *The Tragedy of Francis Bacon*, is, in my opinion, an inconsequential contribution to the controversy. In the chapter on Papermarks, his contention that every fresh device necessitates a new mould (p. 38) is correct, but his deductions are senseless; the fact being that the paper is contributed from very many—mostly foreign—mills. Take one of Caxton's books—say, *The Golden Legend*—and you will find 50 different water-marks in one volume; if all the copies could be examined, probably double or treble the number would be revealed. One hasn't the patience to follow Mr. Bayley's "reasoning": he believes one of the paper-marks (No. 55) to be Rosicrucian—it is the Divine monogram, and traceable to the first century. No. 14, the "fool's-cap," gives the name to a size of paper still extant—so of the vase, or "pott." The symbols are allusive, heraldic, or "canting," mostly emblematic, or in rebus form. That is all. What more natural for the paper-maker *Lile* than to take the Fleur-de-lys for his trade symbol? With respect to printers' headlines, tail-pieces, etc., they were (and are) simply fancy types used for decorative purposes. The oak, and its fruit the acorn—the rose, Tudor or otherwise, the lily, typifying our conquest of France, only erased from the Royal Arms *temp*. George III., would all, from a national standpoint, become the commonest form of ornament, and each, in its turn, lend itself to the fancy of the designer, who, Mr. Bayley would have us think, were all under the direction of Francis Bacon, who wove a wonderful story by this puerile means. As for the printers' "hieroglyphics," as Mr. Bayley calls them, they have been used almost from the invention of the art to the present time. Amongst publishers, too, they are common. The printer of *The Tragedy of Sir Francis Bacon* employs one: a lion supporting the trade symbol of Aldus. I have not consulted Mr. Whittingham, but (if he knows anything at all about it) he would probably say the device signifies that he is the English successor of the Venetian printer!

So far as Shakespeare's handwriting is concerned, I do not propose at the present moment to go beyond the opinion of Spedding. It would profit nothing to enter into a discussion on the subject until one has something tangible in the way of evidence to offer. Shakespeare's Will, for instance, has always been regarded as a witness for the Baconian case, but if the result of the investigations I am prosecuting confirm my suspicions, it will become a piece of important evidence for Shakespeare. The *bona-fides* of this Will have always appeared to be more than questionable, and I am hopeful of being in a position shortly to connect it with the great fraud which I am satisfied has been perpetrated by Bacon.

FRONTISPIECE TO SYLVA SYLVARUM

THE BI-LITERAL CIPHER.

THE most interesting feature of the Bacon-Shakespeare controversy at the present moment is the alleged discovery by Mrs. Elizabeth Wells Gallup, of Detroit, U.S.A., of a bi-literal cipher by Bacon, which appears in no fewer than forty-five books, published between 1591 and 1628. Mrs. Gallup was assisting Dr. Orville W. Owen (also of Detroit, U.S.A.), in the preparation of the later books of his *Sir Francis Bacon's Cipher Story*, and in the study of the "great word cipher," discovered by Dr. Owen, when she became convinced that the very full explanation found in *De Augmentis Scientiarum* of the bi-literal method of cipher-writing, was something more than a mere treatise on the subject. She applied the rules given to the peculiarly italicised words, and "letters in two forms," as they appear in the photographic facsimile of the 1623 folio edition of the Shakespeare plays. The surprising disclosures that resulted from the experiment, sent her to the original editions of Bacon's known works, and from those to all the authors whose books Bacon claimed as his own. The bi-literal cipher, according to Mrs. Gallup, held true in every instance, and she is fully entitled to have her discovery thoroughly investigated before it is condemned as a "pure invention." Mrs. Gallup solemnly declares her translation to be "absolutely veracious," and until it is authoritatively declared that the bi-literal cipher does not exist in the works in which she professes to have traced it, I am not prepared to question her *bonâ fides*. Her conclusions are absurd, but her premises may be proved to be impregnable. She is convinced of the soundness of her discoveries, and she forthwith leaps to the conclusion that "the proofs are overwhelming and irresistible, that Bacon was the author of the delightful lines attributed to Spenser—the fantastic conceits of Peele and Greene—the historical romances of Marlowe—the immortal plays and poems put forth in Shakespeare's name—as well as the *Anatomy of Melancholy* of Burton." Mrs. Gallup shows scant appreciation of the illimitable genius she claims for Bacon in this sentence.

The inaccurately described bi-literal cipher, which Bacon, who claims to have invented it, explained with great elaboration in his *De Augmentis Scientiarum*, has nothing whatever to do with the composition or the wording of the works in which it is said to exist. It depends not on the author, but on the printer. It is altogether a matter of typography. One condition alone is necessary—control over the printing, so as to ensure its being done from specially marked manuscripts, or altered in proof. It shall, as Bacon says, be performed thus:—"First let all the letters of the alphabet, by transposition, be resolved into two letters only—hence bi-literal—for the transposition of two letters by five placings will be sufficient for 32 differences, much more than 24, which is the number of the alphabet. The example of such an alphabet is on this wise:—

A aaaaa	I or J abaaa	R baaaa
B aaaab	K abaab	S baaab
C aaaba	L ababa	T baaba
D aaabb	M ababb	U or V baabb
E aabaa	N abbaa	W babaa
F aabab	O abbab	X babab
G aabba	P abbba	Y babba
H aabbb	Q abbbb	Z babbb

For the purpose of introducing this alphabet into the book which is to contain the secret message, certain letters are taken to stand for "a's" and others for "b's." In Bacon's illustration, he employed two different founts of italic type, using the letters of fount "a" to stand for "a's," and the letters of fount "b" to stand for "b's." Bacon takes the word "fuge" to exhibit the application of the alphabet, thus:—

F	U	G	E.
aabab	baabb	aabba	aabaa

The word is enfolded, as an illustration, in the sentence *Manere te volo donec venero*, as follows:—

MANERE TE VOLO DONEC VENERO.

aabab	baabb	aabba	aabaa
F.	U.	G.	E.

A more ample example of the cipher is given on the page which is here reproduced from Mrs. Gallup's book. The work in which the "interiour" letter is enfolded is the first *Epistle of Cicero*, and the cipher letter it contains is as follows:

All is lost. Mindarus is killed. The soldiers want food.
We can neither get hence nor stay longer here.

THE BI-LITERAL CIPHER.

Cicero's First Epistle.

In all duty or rather piety towards you, I satisfy everybody except myself. Myself I never satisfy. For so great are the services which you have rendered me, that, seeing you did not rest in your endeavours on my behalf till the thing was done, I feel as if life had lost all its sweetness, because I cannot do as much in this cause of yours. The occasions are these: Ammonius, the king's ambassador, openly besieges us with money. The business is carried on through the same creditors who were employed in it when you were here &c.

(NOTE)—This Translation from Spedding, Ellis & Heath Ed.

Bacon had a three-fold motive for putting his cipher into every book of merit that was published in his day. In the first place, it allowed him to claim the authorship of the book. In the second, in Mrs. Gallup's own words, "it was the means of conveying to a future time the truth which was being concealed from the world concerning himself—his right to be King of England—secrets of State regarding Queen Elizabeth—his mother—and other prominent characters of that day—the correction of English history in important particulars, the exposure of the wrongs that had been put upon him;" and, equally important, thirdly, of publishing his version of the wrongs he had done to others, and to Essex in particular. Concerning the amazing diversity of style displayed in the many works, he says in his cipher: "I varied my stile to suit men, since no two shew the same taste and like imagination...." "When I have assum'd men's names, th' next step is to create for each a stile naturall to the man that yet should let my owne bee seene, as a thrid of warpe in my entire fabricke." His explanation of the diversity of merit that is displayed in the works of Robert Greene and of Shakespeare, is not less interesting and instructive. "It shall bee noted in truth that some (plays) greatly exceede their fellowes in worth, and it is easily explained. Th' theame varied, yet was always a subject well selected to convey the secret message. Also the plays being given out as tho'gh written by the actor, to whom each had bin consign'd, turne one's genius suddainlie many times to suit th' new man."

"In this actour that wee now emploie (the cipher appears in the 1611 quarto edition of *Hamlet*), is a wittie veyne different from any formerly employ'd. [Bacon appears to have forgotten that he employed the 'masque' of Shakespeare in the quarto editions of *Richard II.* (1598), *Midsummer Night's Dream, Much Ado About Nothing, The Merchant of Venice* (1600), and of *King Lear, Henry V.* (1608), and *Pericles* (1609)]. In truth it suiteth well with a native spirrit, humourous and grave by turnes in ourself. Therefore, when wee create a part that hath him in minde, th' play is correspondingly better therefor."

In the cipher story which is found by Mrs. Gallup in *Titus Andronicus*, Bacon again recurs to the superior merit of the plays put forth in Shakespeare's name, and he extols the merits of Shakespeare as an interpreter of these dramas:—

"We can win bayes, lawrell gyrlo'ds and renowne, and we can raise a shining monumente which shale not suffer the hardly wonne, supremest, crowning glory to fade. Nere shal the lofty and wide-reaching honor that such workes as these bro't us bee lost whilst there may even a work bee found to afforde opportunity to actors—who may play those powerful parts which are now soe greeted with great acclayme—to winne such names and honours as Wil Shakespear, o' The Glob' so well did win, acting our dramas.

"That honour must to earth's final morn yet follow him, but al fame won from th' authorshippe (supposed) of our plays must in good time—after our owne worke, putting away its vayling disguises, standeth forth as you (the decipherer) only know it—bee yeelded to us."

If Mr. Mallock reposes any confidence in his Bacon—according to Mrs. Gallup—he must at once withdraw his description of Shakespeare as a "notorious-

THE BI-LITERAL CIPHER. 47

ly ill-educated actor." Bacon himself, in the foregoing, acknowledges that Will Shakespeare derived a well-won reputation and honours by acting in his dramas. At the same time Bacon is confident that the dramas will win for him, as author, "supremest, crowning, and unfading glory."

Here, almost at the outset of these cipher revelations, we are met by a passage, plausible in itself, but which, read in the light of our knowledge of Bacon's doubts upon the permanency of the English language, calls for careful consideration. Bacon rested his fame upon his Latin writings. He wrote always for the appreciation of posterity. As he advanced in years, he appears, says Abbott, to have been more and more impressed with the hopelessness of any expectations of lasting fame or usefulness based upon English books. He believed implicitly that posterity would not preserve works written in the modern languages—"for these modern languages will at one time or other play the bank-rowtes (bankrupts) with books." Of his Latin translation of the *Advancement of Learning*, he said, "It is a book I think will live, and be a citizen of the world, as English books will not," and he predicted that the Latin volume of his *Essays* would "last as long as books shall last." So confident was he that his writings would achieve immortality, that he dedicated his *Advancement of Learning* to the King, in order that the virtues and mental qualities of his Majesty might be handed down to succeeding ages in "some solid work, fixed memorial, and immortal monument." Bacon's pride in his work was monumental, his "grasp on futurity" was conceived in a spirit of "magnificent audacity;" every scrap of his writings was jealously preserved and robed in the time-resisting garments of a dead language. Is it conceivable in this magnificent egoist that he should have displayed such gross carelessness, such wanton unconcern in his plays that, but for the labours of a couple of actors in collecting and arranging them, they would have been utterly lost? It is simply incredible that Bacon should have based his anticipation of immortality upon plays which for years were tossed about the world in pirated and mutilated editions, and in many instances, until the issue of the first folio in 1623, existed only in the form of the actor's prompt books. The sixteen plays, in quarto, which were in print in 1616, were published without the co-operation of the author. They were to win for their author unfading glory, yet he was at no pains to collect them. The first folio was printed from the acting versions in use by the company with which Shakespeare had been associated, and the editorial duties were undertaken by two of Shakespeare's friends and fellow actors, whose motives rather than their literary fitness for the task call for commendation. It was dedicated to two noblemen, with whom, so far as we know, Bacon had no social or political intercourse.

Mr. Theobald considers that Bacon's "confident assurance of holding a lasting place in literature," his anticipation of immortality, could only have been advanced by the man who voiced the same conviction in the Shakespeare *Sonnets*. The deduction is based on arbitrary conjecture, and a limited acquaintance with the literary conceits of the time. But Shakespeare claimed as his medium of immortality the language which Bacon predicted could not endure.

FRONTISPIECE TO NOVUM ORGANUM

"So long as men can breathe, or eyes can see—
So long lives this, and this gives life to Thee,"

wrote Shakespeare. This was English, the purest and the sweetest that tongue ever uttered, and Bacon was dressing his thoughts in Latin that they might outlive the language which Shakespeare wrote. Ronsard and Desportes, in France, and in

England, Drayton, Daniel, and, indeed, all the Elizabethan poets, had made the topic a commonplace. In his *Apologie for Poetrie*, Sir Philip Sidney wrote that it was the custom of poets "to tell you that they will make you immortal by their verses," and both Shakespeare and Bacon adopted the current conceit when they referred to the "eternising" faculty of their literary effusions. It is not claimed by, or for, Bacon that he was the author of Drayton's *Idea* or Daniel's *Delia*, but if Mr. Theobald's style of reasoning is to be taken at his own valuation, the master of Gorhambury, and none other, was responsible for the poetic output of both these singers.

BACON'S "STERNE AND TRAGICLE HISTORY."

We are assured by another Baconian student that the Shakespeare plays were not an end, but merely a means to an end, the end being the revelation of Bacon's history, and the composition of further plays and poems from the material which he had warehoused in the dramas attributed to Shakespeare and other authors. The initial, and most important fact which Mrs. Gallup's deciphered story reveals, is, not that Francis Bacon was the author of Shakespeare's plays, but that he was the legitimate son of Queen Elizabeth, by Robert Dudley, afterwards Earl of Leicester. The disclosure is so startling, so quaint, so incredible, and withal so interesting, that the revelation both appeals to and outrages our credulity. From our knowledge of Elizabeth and of Bacon, we can more readily believe that the Queen was the mother of Bacon, than that Bacon was the father of Shakespeare's plays. At Gorhambury is to be seen a pair of oil paintings, by Hilliard, of Elizabeth and Leicester. The pictures are a match in size, style, and treatment. The doublet in which Leicester is portrayed is of the same material as that of the gown in which the Queen is represented. Moreover, they were a present from Elizabeth to Sir Nicholas Bacon, the foster father of Francis, who signs his cipher revelations, "Francis First of England," "Francis Bacon (Rightful) R," "F.B. or T." or "Francis of E.", as the humour seized him.

The deciphered secret story, the "sterne and tragicle" history of Bacon's political wrongs commences in the first edition of Edmund Spenser's *Complaints* (1590 and 1591); but it was not until the *Faerie Queene* was published (1596) that he appropriates the authorship of Spenser's works. His first care is to establish his claim to the throne:

"Our name is Fr. Bacon, by adoption, yet it shall be different. Being of blood roial (for the Queen, our sov'raigne, who married by a private rite the Earle Leicester—and at a subseque't time, also, as to make surer thereby, without pompe, but i' th' presence o' a suitable number of witnesses, bound herselfe by those hymeneall bands againe—is our mother, and wee were not base-born, or base-begot), we be Tudor, and our stile shall be Francis First, in all proper cours of time, th' King of our realme.

"Early in our life, othe (oath)—or threat as binding in effect as othe, we greatly doubt—was made by our wilful parent concerning succession, and if this cannot bee chang'd, or be not in time withdrawn, we know not how the kingdome shall be obtain'd. But 'tis thus seene or shewn that it can bee noe other's by true desce't, then is set down. To Francis First doth th' crowne, th' honor of our land belong...."

BACON'S "STERNE AND TRAGICLE HISTORY." 51

GORHAMBURY, A.D. 1568.

GORHAMBURY, A.D. 1795.

GORHAMBURY, A.D. 1821.

Thus Bacon states his case, and through the succeeding 368 pages of Mrs. Gallup's book he repeats the assertion *ad nauseam*. He makes no attempt to prove his claim—he early allows it to be understood that he is unable to verify his asseverations, nor does he explain how or why his name should be Tuder, or Tidder. As the son of Lord Robert Dudley, he would be a Dudley. The circumstantial evidence with which he supports his case is interesting, but valueless; his conclusions are unproven, his facts are something more than shaky. But let us pursue the story:

"We, by men call'd Bacon, are sonne of the Sov'raigne, Queene Elizabeth, who confin'd i' th' Tow'r, married Ro. D."

Elizabeth, it appears, was once "so mad daring" as to dub Bacon, "as a sonne of Follie," to "th' courageous men of our broadland." But—

"No man hath claime to such pow'r as some shal se in mighty England, after th' decease of Virgin Queene E— — by dull, slow mortalls, farre or near, loved, wooed like some gen'rously affected youth-loving mayden, whylst she is both wife to th' noble lord that was so sodainly cut off in his full tide and vigour of life and mothe'—in such way as th' women of the world have groaninglie bro't foorth, and must whilst Nature doth raigne—of two noble sonnes, Earle of Essex, trained up by Devereux, and he who doth speake to you, th' foster sonne of two wel fam'd frie'ds o' th' Que., Sir Nichola' Bacon, her wo'thie adviser and counsellor, and that partne' of loving labor and dutie, my most loved Lady Anne Bacon...."

"... My mother Elizabeth ... join'd herselfe in a union with Robert Dudley whilst th' oath sworne to one as belov'd yet bound him. I have bene told hee aided in th' removall of this obstructio', when turni'g on that narrowe treach'rous step, as is naturall, shee lightly leaned upon th' raile, fell on th' bricks—th' paving of a court—and so died."

"In such a sonne," Bacon proceeds, "th' wisest our age thus farr hath shewen—pardon, prithee, so u'seemly a phrase, I must speake it heere—th' mother should lose selfish vanitie, and be actuated only by a desire for his advancement."

Bacon is confident that the Queen would have acknowledged his claims but for the advice of a "fox seen at our court in th' form and outward appearance of a man named Robbert Cecill, the hunchback," who poisoned Elizabeth's mind against her "sonne of Follie." Both "Francis Tudor" (or Tidder), and his brother Essex, the "wrong'd enfan's of a Queenee," learned that their "royall aspirations" were to receive "a dampening, a checke soe great, it co'vinc'd both, wee were hoping for advanceme't we might never attaine."

The "royall aspirations" of the Earl of Essex were cut short by the sentence of death that was passed upon him by "that *mère* and my owne counsel. Yet this truth must at some time be knowne; had not I allow'd myselfe to give some countenance to th' arraignement, a subsequent triall, as wel as th' sentence, I must have lost th' life that I held so pricelesse." And Bacon, or Francis Tidder, solaces himself, and condones his part in the deed with the reflection that, "Life to a schola' is but a pawne for mankind."

Queen Elizabeth, Bacon tells us, though already wedded "secretly to th' Earle, my father, at th' Tower of London, was afterwards married at the house of Lord P— —...."

Briefly, then, we have it, on the authority of the cipher translation, that "Bacon was the son of Elizabeth and Robert Dudley, who were married in the Tower between 1554 and 1558. Leicester's wife did not meet with her fatal accident until 1560. Bacon was born in January, 1561. His parents were subsequently re-married, at a date not stated, at the house of Lord P— —."

In 1611 (*Shepheard's Calendar*) Bacon declares "Ended is now my great desire to sit in British throne. Larger worke doth invite my hand than majestie doth offer; to wield th' penne dothe ever require a greater minde then to sway the royall scepter. Ay, I cry to th' Heavenly Ayde, ruling ore all, ever to keepe my soule thus humbled and contente." But in 1613 (*Faerie Queene*), he says, that "in th' secrecy o' my owne bosome, I do still hold to th' faith that my heart has never wholly surrendered, that truth shall come out of error, and my head be crowned ere my line o' life be sever'd. How many times this bright dreeme hath found lodgement in my braine!... It were impossible, I am assurr'd, since witnesses to th' marriage, and to my birth (after a proper length of time) are dead, and the papers certifying their presence being destroyed, yet is it a wrong that will rise, and crye that none can hush." In 1620 (*Novum Organum*) he has lost his "feare, lest my secret bee s'ented forth by some hound o' Queen Elizabeth;" but "the jealousy of the King is to be feared, and that more in dread of effecte on the hearts of the people, then any feare of th' presentation of my claime, knowing as he doth, that all witnesses are dead, and the requir'd documents destroy'd."

Bacon, according to the cipher, was sixteen years of age when he learned the truth of his parentage through the indiscretion of one "th' ladies o' her (the Queen's) train, who foolish to rashnesse did babble such gossip to him as she heard at the Court." Bacon, it seems, taxed the Queen forthwith with her motherhood of him, and Elizabeth, with "much malicious hatred" and "in hastie indignation," said:

"You are my own borne sonne, but you, though truly royall, of a fresh, a masterlie spirit, shall rule not England, or your mother, nor reigne on subjects yet t' bee. I bar from succession forevermore my best beloved first borne that bless'd my unio' with—no, I'll not name him, nor need I yet disclose the sweete story conceal'd thus farre so well, men only guesse it, nor know o' a truth o' th' secret marriages, as rightfull to guard the name o' a Queene, as of a maid o' this realm. It would well beseeme you to make such tales sulk out of sight, but this suiteth not t' your kin'ly spirit. A sonne like mine lifteth hand nere in aide to her who brought him foorth; hee'd rather uplift craven maides who tattle thus whenere my face (aigre enow ev'r, they say) turneth from them. What will this brave boy do? Tell a, b, c's?"

"Weeping and sobbing sore," Bacon hurries to Mistres Bacon's chamber and entreats her to assure him that he is "the sonne of herselfe and her honored husband.... When, therefore, my sweet mother did, weeping and lamenting, owne to me that I was in very truth th' sonne o' th' Queene, I burst into maledictio's 'gainst th' Queene, my fate, life, and all it yieldeth.... I besought her to speak my father's name.... She said, 'He is the Earle of Leicester.... I tooke a solemne oath not to reveale your storie to you, but you may hear my unfinish'd tale to th' end and if you will, go to th' midwife. Th' doctor would be ready also to give proofes of your just right to be named th' Prince of this realm, and heire-apparent to the throne. Nevertheless, Queen Bess did likewise give her solemn oath of bald-faced deniall of her marriage to Lord Leicester, as well as to her motherhood. Her oath, so broken, robs me of a sonne. O Francis, Francis, breake not your mother's hearte. I cannot let you go forth after all the years you have beene the sonne o' my heart. But night is falling. To-day I cannot speak to you of so weighty a matter. This hath mov'd you deeply, and though you now drie your eyes, you have yet many teare marks upon your little cheeks. Go now; do not give it place i' thought or word; a brain-sick woman, though she be a Queene, can take my sonne from me.'" So Bacon leaves her, not to search for the midwife, or cross-question the doctor, but to "dreame of golden scepters, prou' courts, and by-and-bye a crowne on mine innocent brow."

All Bacon's confessions, if true, prove him to have been a bastard, but this logical and inevitable conclusion he repeatedly denies. He claims his mother's name, and for his father, a nobleman whose wife was living at the time of his bigamous marriage with Elizabeth. If the marriage was valid, why were Leicester and the Queen re-married at the house of Lord P., and in what year did the second ceremony take place? But although anti-Baconians maintain that Bacon was not a fool, and therefore could not have seriously advanced such claims; that if he had done so he would have made a more plausible story of his wrongs; that he was not a dunce, and therefore could not have written the "maudlin and illiterate drivel" attributed to him by Mrs. Gallup, it is still inconceivable that this cipher story is a gigantic fraud. Mr. Andrew Lang, who makes no doubt that Mrs. Gallup has honourably carried out her immense task of deciphering, has arrived at the conclusion that Bacon was obviously mad.

BACON, THE AUTHOR OF ALL ELIZABE-THAN-JACOBEAN LITERATURE.

But interesting as it is to find in Bacon yet another and hitherto an unsuspected pretender to the throne of England, his pretensions to the authorship of Shakespeare's plays is a feature of even more dazzling interest. His reasons for denying the authorship while he lived have hitherto demanded a great deal of speculative explanation. The general theory of the Baconites is that Bacon concealed his authorship of the plays because such writing was held in low esteem, or as Mr. Sinnett puts it, Bacon "shrank from compromising his social reputation by any open connection with the despised vocation of the playwright." The difficulty of accepting this assumption has hitherto been found in the fact that there was no reason why Bacon should have confined himself to the writing of plays. In the case of Shakespeare, it was quite understandable, for he was an actor, and the stage was his livelihood. Bacon, on the other hand, had no love for the theatre; he looked upon play-acting as a toy, and masques as things unworthy of serious observations. The tone of his comments is contemptuous, and his criticism discloses a lack of knowledge and interest in the subject. Why should this man, who regarded the stage with ill-concealed repugnance, have written plays which he was ashamed to own, while all imaginative literature was open to him. The stigma which it is erroneously alleged was attached to play-writing was not associated with poetry; if the playwright was under a ban, the poet was on the pedestal. There must have been a more tangible reason for Bacon's concealment, but we have had to wait for Mrs. Gallup's book to disclose it. Bacon's object in writing was to unfold the secrets of his birth and to ventilate his wrongs; he chose plays as his medium because, like Mr. George Bernard Shaw, he found blank verse easier to write than prose. He employed the pseudonyms of Greene and Peele, and the pen name of Marlowe ere taking that of Wm. Shakespeare as his masque or vizard, "that we should remayne unknowne, inasmuch as wee, having worked in drama, history that is most vig'rously suppress, have put ourselfe soe greatly in dange' that a word unto Queene Elizabeth, without doubt, would give us a sodaine horriblle end—an exit without re-entrance—for in truth she is authoress and preserve' of this, our being."

Bacon's first claim to authorship, apart from the works which were issued under his own name, is to be found, according to the cipher, in the 1596 edition of the *Faerie Queene*:

"E. Sp. could not otherwise so easilie atchieve honours that pertyne to ourself. Indeed, this would alone crowne his head, if this were all—I speake not of golden crowne, but of lawrell—for our pen is dipt deepe into th' muses' pure source."

The first mention of Shakespeare as Bacon's masque appears in the J. Roberts' edition (1600) of *Sir John Oldcastle* and *The Merchant of Venice*:

"See or read. In the stage-plaies, two, the oldest or earliest devices prove these twentie plays to have been put upon our stage by the actor that is suppos'd to sell dramas of value, yet 'tis rightlie mine owne labour."

In the *Advancement of Learning* (1605) Bacon extends his claim to embrace the works of Robert Greene, Peele, Marlowe, and Ben Jonson:

"My stage plaies have all been disguis'd (to wit, many in Greene's name, or in Peele's, Marlowe's, a fewe, such as the Queen's Masques and others of this kind published for me by Jonson, my friend and co-worker) since I relate a secret history therein, a story of so sterne and tragick qualite, it ille suited my lighte' verse, in the earlier works."

The only other persons who are permitted the privilege of communicating with posterity, through the medium of the cipher, are Bacon's "friends and co-workers," Ben Jonson and William Rawley. In the folio edition of Jonson's plays (1616) at Bacon's "constantly urged request," Jonson, who had his friend's "fame in heart as much as my honour and dignitie," writes to the decipherer:

"It shall be noted, indeed, when you uncover his stile, my works do not all come from mine owne penne, for I shall name to you some plays that come forth fro' Sir F. Bacon, his worthy hand or head, I bein' but the masque behind which he was surely hid. Th' play entitled *Sejanus* was his drama, and th' King's, Queen's, Prince's Entertainments; the *Queen's Masques* are his, as also th' short *Panegyre*."

But we learn that, in addition to Jonson, "my foster-brother Anthony, my owne brother Robert, Ben Jonson, my friend, adviser and assistant, and our private secretary," were also "cogniza't of the work," and indeed after Bacon's death in 1626, William Rawley, his private secretary, took up the cipher story, and completed it in Burton's *Anatomy of Melancholy*, and in the 1635 editions of *Sylva Sylvarum* and the *New Atlantis*. It has been objected that Bacon could not have dropped the cipher into books published after his death, but this objection "vanishes into invisibility," as Mr. Theobald would say, when we remember that faithful old Rawley was living long after Bacon's work had been "cut short by th' sickel o' death." He bobs up serenely in *Sylva Sylvarum*, drops in another thirty pages of Bacon's cipher lamentations, and winds up with a dozen lines of his own "to speak of th' errata." This last instalment was, it may be assumed, written prior to 1626, and entrusted to Rawley to make use of on the first opportunity, *i.e.*, as soon as he could obtain command of the proofs of another book.

In the first folio, published twenty years after the death of Elizabeth, Bacon still appears to be affrighted by the memory of the Queen; his life would still be forfeit if his identity were discovered, "since she is my mother;" but in his valedictory address to his decipherer, he declares that it is "not feare, but disstaste of th' unseemly talk and much curiosity of the many who read these cipher histories, that makes him still desirous to preserving his incognito."

SHAKESPEARE. THE DROESHOUT ETCHING,
from the 1623 Folio Edition.

To the Reader.

This Figure, that thou here seest put,
It was for gentle Shakespeare cut;
Wherein the Grauer had a strife
with Nature, to out-doo the life:
O, could he but haue drawne his wit
As well in brasse, as he hath hit
His face; the Print would then surpasse
All, that was euer writ in brasse.
But, since he cannot, Reader, looke
Not on his Picture, but his Booke.

                                                       B. I.

"My time of feare went from me with my greatness, but I still wish to avoid many questionings—and much suspicion, perchance on the side of the King, in his owne prope' person. I have neede of the very caution which kept these secrets from the many, when my mother made me swear secrecy, and my life was the forfeit; nor may I now speake openly, yet many men for a kingdom would break their oathes."

It is possible that Bacon may have considered that "since witnesses to th' marriage and to my birth ... are dead, and the papers certifying their presence" were destroyed, he would have a better chance of obtaining credence for his story a few centuries hence than in his own day. His belief in the credulity of posterity did not desert him:

"But my kingdome is in immortall glory among men from generatio' unto coming generations. An unending fame will crowne my browe, and it is farre better worthe in any true thinking mind, I am assured, than many a crowne which kings do have set on with shewe and ceremonie. Yet when I have said it, my heart is sad for the great wrong that I must for ever endure."

Bacon appears to have foreseen that some future sceptic would question the justice of his claims; would ask, for instance, how the hand that wrote *Macbeth* and *The Tempest*, came to produce such comparatively indifferent stuff as *A Quip for an Upstart Courtier*, and he meets the anticipated question with the following explanation:—

"It shall bee noted in truth that some greatly exceede their fellowes in worth, and it is easily explained. Th' theame varied, yet was always a subject well selected to convey the secret message. Also the plays being given out as tho'gh written by the actor to whom each had been consigned, turne one's genius suddainlie many times to suit th' new man.

"In this actour that wee now emploie, is a wittie vayne different from any formerly employed. In truth it suiteth well with a native spirrit, humorous and grave by turnes in ourselfe. Therefore when we create a part that hath him in minde th' play is correspondingly better therefor. It must be evident ... that these later dramas (this cipher message is in the 1611 quarto of *Hamlet*) are superior in nearlie all those scenes where our genius hath swaie"....

Over and over again, with almost childish iteration, the cipher repeats the names of the authors whose works he claims as his own:

"Spenser, Greene, Peele, Marlowe have sold me theirs (their names)—two or three others I have assumed upon certaine occasions such as this (Ben Jonson's *Masques*), besides th' one I beare among men."...

"My plaies are not yet finisht, but I intend to put forth severall soone. However, bi-literall work requiring so much time, it will readily be seene that there is much to doe aftee a booke doth seeme to be ready for the presse, and I could not say when other plays will come out. The next volume will be under W. Shakespeare's name. As some which have now beene produced have borne upon the title page his name though all are my owne work, I have allow'd it to stand on manie others which I myselfe regard as equall in merite."

"My next work is not begun here: much of it shall bee found in th' playes o' Shakespeare which have not yet come out. We having put forth a numbe' of plays i' his theatre, shall continue soe doing since we doe make him th' thrall to our will. Our name never accompanieth anie play, but it frequently appeareth plainly in cipher for witty minds to transla'e from Latine and Greeke...."

"This history (*The Tragical Historie of the Earl of Essex*) is contained (*i.e.*, hidden in cipher) in some stage plays that came out in Shakespeare's name. Ere long there will be many of like stile, purpose and scope added thereto, which shall both ayd and instruct you in th' work. This should make it cleare, *e.g.*, sixty stage-plays which, in varyi'g stiles that are contrary to my owne well-known stile of expression, whylst for more of our lighter work an impenetrable mask, for a history, much too varied: hence these great plays have been devis'd which, being similar, often held this inne' history therein unsuspected...."

"Several comedies, which be now strangers, as might be said, bearing at th' most such titles 'mongst the plaiers as they would remember, but th' author's name in disguise, if it bee seen at all, will, as soone as may be found toward and propitious, be publisht by Shakespeare, *i.e.*, in his name, having masqued thus manie of the best plaies that we have beene able to produce. To these we are steadily making additions, writing from two to six stage plays every year...."

"All that learne that I, who accompte th' truth better than wicked vanitie, publish'd manie late playes under other cognomen will think the motive some distaste of the stage. In noe respect is it true...." His real reason is, firstly, that "all men who write stage-playes are held in co'tempte," and, secondly, the plays are employed to "send out much hidden dang'rous matter." "In my plays matters are chosen not alone for value as a subject to heare and no longer heed. Each play is the meane or th' medium, by which cipher histories are sent forth."

"Severall small works under no name wonne worthy praise; next in Spenser's name, also, they ventured into an unknowne world. When I, at length, having written in diverse stiles, found three who, for sufficient reward in gold added to an immediate renowne as good pens, willingly put forth all workes which I had compos'd I was bolder...."

"Th' evidence such plays give of being from the brayne of one who hath for manie years made himself acquainted with th' formes and th' methode—or art—of this dramatick or representative poetry, maketh also my claime to other workes, which have beene publisht in various names, undeniable. The worke, despight a variety of styles, is mine owne...."

"So few (plays) can bee put forth as first written without a slighte revision, and many new being also made ready, my penne hath little or noe rest. I am speaking of those plaies that were suppos'd Wm. Shakespeare's...."

"... small portions (of the cipher story) being used at one time, sometimes in our Spenser's name, Marlowe's, Peele's, and Shakespeare's, anon Greene's, mine, also Ben Jonson's, affording our diverse masques another colour, as 'twere, to baffle all seekers, to which we shall add Burton's...."

"Th' worke beareth the title of the *Anatomy of Melancholy*, and will bee put forth by Burton."

SHAKESPEARE. THE CHANDOS PORTRAIT.

Here is Bacon's announcement of the publication of the First Folio:

"In our plaies ... being in the name of a man not living, there is still more of this secret historie.... We have not lost that maske tho' our Shakespeare no longer liveth, since twoo others, fellowes of our play actor—who would, we doubt not, publish those plays—would disguise our work as well...."

"Our plaies are of diverse kindes—historie, comedie, and tragedie. Many are upon th' stage, but those already put forth in Wm. Shakespeare's name, we doe nothing doubt, have won a lasting fame,—comedy, th' historick drama and tragedy, are alike in favour...."

"My best playes, at present, as William Shakespeare's work fost'red, will as soone as one more plaie be completed, weare a fine but yet a quiet dresse, as is seemely in plaies of as much valew and dignity as sheweth cleerly therein, and be put foorth in folio enlarged and multiplyed as th' history conceal'd within th' comedies, histories, or tragedies required."

Then follows a number of further recapitulations of his masques:

"Francis of Verulam is author of all the plays heretofore published by Marlowe, Greene, Peele, Shakespeare, and of the two-and-twenty now put out for the first time. Some are altered to continue his history...."

"Next write a comedy, a quaint device for making knowne th' men that do give, lend, sell, or in anie othe' waye, have put me into possession of their names. These I have us'd as disguises that my name might not bee seen attached to any poem, stage-play, or anie of th' light workes o' this day...."

"As I have often said ... you have poems and prose workes on divers theames in all such various stiles, as are put before th' world as Greene's, as Shakespeare's, Burto's, as Peele's, Spenser's, as Marlowe's, as Jonso' dramas ... for I varied my stile to suit different men, since no two shew th' same taste and like imagination...."

"Any play publisht as Marlowe's, came from th' same source as all which you will now work out...."

"Greene, Spense', Peele, Shakespeare, Burton, and Marley, as you may somewhere see it, or, as it is usually given, Marlowe, have thus farre been my masques...."

"A few workes also beare th' name o' my friend, Ben Jonson—these are *Sejanus* and th' *Masques*, used to conceale the Iliads chiefly and to make use o' my newe cipher...."

"I masqued manie grave secrets in my poems which I have publisht, now as Peele's or Spenser's, now as my owne, then againe in th' name of authours, so cald, who plac'd workes of mixt sort before a reading world, prose and poetry. To Robt. Greene did I entruste most of that work...."

Bacon has limited our speculations upon the extent of his literary work by definitely mentioning the works which he wrote in a cipher discovered by Dr. Owen:

> "We will enumerate them by their whole titles
> From the beginning to the end: William Shakespeare,
> Robert Greene, George Peele, and Christopher Marlowe's
> Stage plays; *The Faerie Queen, Shepherd's Calendar,*
> And all the works of Edmund Spenser;
> *The Anatomy of Melancholy* of Robert Burton,

*The History of Henry VII., The Natural History,
The Interpretation of Nature, The Great Instauration,
Advancement of Learning, The De Augmentis Scientiarum,
Our Essays,* and all the other works of our own."

Even when we note that the *Advancement* and *De Augmentis* are the English and Latin versions of the same work—a fact that Dr. Owen appears to have overlooked—Mr. Theobald must acknowledge that this represents a very fair literary output, but it does not form the full list of his works. The names of his cipher or interiour works, are enumerated by Mrs. Gallup:

"There are five histories as followes: *The Life o' Elizabeth, The Life of Essex, The White Rose o' Britaine, The Life and Death of Edward Third, The Life of Henry th' Seventh;* five tragedies: *Mary Queene o' Scots, Robert th' Earl o' Essex* (my late brother), *Robert th' Earle o' Leicester* (my late father), *Death o' Marlowe, Ann Bullen;* three comedies: *Seven Wise Men o' th' West, Solomon th' Second, The Mouse-Trap.*"

BACON AND "DIVINE AIDE."

BACON himself appears to have been struck with the immensity of his production, and he cast about for some plausible explanation that would justify it in the eyes of his twentieth century admirers. Human endurance and fecundity would, he foresaw, be regarded as unequal to the strain—Divine assistance alone could make so colossal a task possible:

"Whosoever may question assertions that tend to shew y' mankinde evidences of a Divine thought interfusing th' human minde, hath but to prove it by experiment. He would not bee ready to cavil, or laugh to scorn this assertion, which I may repeat anon, that Divine aide was given me in my work. I have, at th' least, accomplished a great work in fewe yeares, work of such a difficult nature that no one hand could accomplish, except other than myselfe upheld or directed it." And "anon," he repeats, "surely my hand and braine have but short rest. I firmly believe it were not in the power of humane beings to do anie more than I have done, yet I am but partlie satisfied."

These excerpts, which have been given at some length, disclose not only the exact nature and extent of the alleged claims, but the style and manner in which they are couched. There is nothing of the literary polish and elegance in the cipher writing which we find in all of Bacon's acknowledged works, but taking into consideration the difficulties of dropping the cipher into the books in which it is said to appear, and the even greater difficulties of interpreting it, it seems manifestly unfair to dismiss the entire thing as an imposture on that account. Mr. Mallock's contention is that Mrs. Gallup's theory is sufficiently plausible to merit it an unprejudiced investigation. If the cipher proves to be altogether false, the manner in which it has been elaborated will, Mr. Mallock submits, form a curious incident in literary history; while should it prove true, it will be more curious still. Apart from the cipher, Mr. Sinnett declares, there are floods of reasons for disbelieving that Shakespeare could have written the plays. Mr. Sinnett, and the other leaders of the Baconian cult, do not appear to see that if their theory is to outlast the present controversy, the cipher business must be thrown overboard forthwith.

As Mr. William Archer has said with reference to these ciphers, the point at issue is as plain as a pike-staff. We are not concerned, while we deal with this phase of the subject, in the verbal parallels between Shakespeare's writings and those of Bacon, nor with the vehemently expressed conviction of students and scholars that Bacon did not write *Shakespeare*. All we desire to know is whether the ciphers which Mrs. Gallup and Dr. Owen contend are contained in certain books (the *First Folio Shakespeare* among others) really exist. Mr. Mallock says that until an examination by experts in typography has negatived this theory, he is inclined to believe it. His position is unassailable. Nothing further can be argued or asserted (with conviction) until a committee of experts have made their report. If they declare that the cipher has no foundation in fact, the students who have carefully perused Mrs. Gallup's great work—great invention it will then be—and Dr. Owen's many volumes of badly-constructed, ridiculous plays and poems, will give both Mrs. Gallup and Dr. Owen credit for a veritable triumph of misapplied energy and endurance—for having conceived a masterpiece of diabolical inventiveness, for having revealed a perfect genius for the perpetration of literary fraud.

Personally, I do not expect to learn that they will be convicted of the possession of such an exceptional gift of deception. Their labours smack of honesty; their conclusions betray an ingenuous credulity that calls for respect. It will, indeed, surprise most people who have made a study of their works, if it is proved that the cipher they claim to have discovered, and manipulated with such marvellous results, is a myth. But assuming that a properly-constituted committee did declare that the cipher was to be found in all the books indicated, and that the investigation corroborated the revelations made by Mrs. Gallup and Dr. Owen, there would still remain the question as to who concealed the statements in the different volumes, and whether there is any truth in them.

I think, nay I claim, that in the event of the cipher being verified, and the translations being confirmed, that (*a*) The cipher could have been introduced by no other man than Bacon; and that (*b*) The whole of the statements found therein are false from beginning to end. In a searching investigation into the cipher undertaken by a correspondent of the *Times*, a single page of the cipher was tested, but the test is not, as the *Times* claims for it, entirely convincing. The method of investigation employed is excellent. A greatly enlarged photograph is taken of a page from the *Epistle Dedicatory* to the *Ruine of Time* in the 1591 edition of Spenser's *Complaints*, and the "A" and "B" letters which Mrs. Gallup herself assigns to the parts respectively are cut out and arranged in parallel columns. When these two sets of letters are seen side by side it would, indeed, be difficult for the untrained eye to distinguish any marks of dissimilarity between them. But as Mr. Mallock tells us, "although even the naked eye can be soon trained to perceive that in many cases the letters belong to different founts, yet these differences are of so minute a kind that in other cases they allude the eye without the aid of a magnifying glass; and even with the aid of a magnifying glass, the eye of the amateur, at all events, remains doubtful, and unable to assign the letters to this alphabet or to that." The correspondent of the *Times* leads us to infer that he has been unable to verify the existence of the cipher in the page he has tested, and Mr. Lee has declared, without hesitation, that the cipher does not exist in the Shakespeare First Folio. On the other hand, Mr. Mallock had little difficulty in distinguishing the different founts in the facsimiles from the *Novum Organum* and Spenser's *Complaints*. He experimented with a large number of passages, and comparing his interpretation with that of Mrs. Gallup, he found that it coincided with hers, sometimes in four cases out of seven, and not infrequently in five. "It appears to me," Mr. Mallock writes, "to be almost inconceivable that multiplied coincidences such as these can be the work of chance, or that they can originate otherwise than in the fact that in these pages at all events—the preface to the *Novum Organum*, printed in 1620, and in the Dedication of Spenser's *Complaints*, printed in 1591—a bi-literal cipher exists, in both cases the work of Bacon; and if such a cipher really exists here, the probabilities are overwhelming that Mrs. Gallup is right, and that we shall find it existing in the first folio of Shakespeare also."

SHAKESPEARE AND BACON IN COLLABO-RATION.

BACON's ciphers, which were, according to the evidence adduced from the bi-literal, six in number, grew one out of the other. Bacon evidently expected the bi-literal to be discovered first, for in this cipher he explains the word-cipher, in which his hidden, or "interiour" works are concealed. Dr. Owen discovered this word-cipher without the aid of the bi-literal, and by following its directions he has deciphered over a thousand pages of blank verse, comprising *Letters to the Decipherer, A Description of Queen Elizabeth,* a poem entitled *The Spanish Armada, An Account of Bacon's Life in France,* and several plays. In the *Epistle to the Decipherer,* Bacon says, "For thirty-three years have we gone in travail, with these, the children of our wit," and proceeds to adjure the unknown to

> "Sware by my sword never to speak of this
> That you have found while we do live;"

and again—

> "Sweare never to publish that we conceal under the names
> Of others our own till we are dead,
> Sweare never to reveal the secret cipher words
> That guide your steps from part to part,
> Nor how it is gathered, joined or put together,
> Till we be dead, so help you God!"

The chief point to be noted about these cipher stories, biographies and plays is that they are built up of quotations from the works of all the authors whose writings Bacon claims to be his own. Dr. Owen asks us, in all seriousness, to believe that Bacon composed the plays of Shakespeare, Marlowe, Peel, and Greene, and the poems by Spenser, as they appear in the cipher translation, and that he subsequently "decomposed and composed them again" for circulation in his own day, under the names of the various authors who acted as his masques. "When deciphered and replaced in their original form," Dr. Owen asserts, "they *mean something* which they *do not* in the plays." Such a statement, as anyone can prove by turning to these curious deciphered books, is both fallacious and absurd.

Let us see what these passages which *mean nothing* in the plays mean in the cipher stories. The pledge which Hamlet imposes upon Horatio and Marcellus after the interview with the ghost is a serviceable case in point. Hamlet's words are almost too familiar to need repeating:

> "So help you mercy, that how strange

SHAKESPEARE AND BACON IN COLLABORATION. 67

> Or odd soe'er I bear myself—
> As I, perchance, hereafter shall think meet
> To put an antic disposition on—
> That you, at such times seeing me, never shall,
> With arms encumber'd thus, or this head shake,
> Or by pronouncing of some doubtful phrase,
> As 'Well, well, we know;'—or 'We could, and if we would;'
> Or 'If we list to speak;'—or, 'There be, an if they might:'—
> Or such ambiguous giving out, to note
> That you know aught of me;—This not to do,
> So grace and mercy at your most need help you,
> Swear."

No one can question the fitness and perfect appropriateness of the foregoing passage in *Hamlet*, but it is doubtful if anybody, other than Dr. Owen, will recognise their cogency when they are addressed by Bacon to his unknown decipherer.

Bacon declares that Bottom's recital of his dream, which commences,

> "The eye of man hath not heard,
> The ear of man hath not seen,"

is

> "Simply and plainly, the ingenious means of writing
> Without creating suspicion;"

and he goes on to explain that the decipherer can, by changing

> "The words from one end to another, make it read aright."

Bacon heartens his timorous decipherer with the words, "Be thou not, therefore, afraid of greatness"—the greatness that he will attain as the reward of his decipherations. "Some," he assures the unknown, in the memorable words, "have greatness thrust upon them," and he further reminds him that

> "There is a tide in the affairs of man,
> Which taken at the flood,
> Leads on to glorious fortune."

"Nature and fortune joined to make you great," Bacon tells his decipherer, from the text of *King John*, and one can almost imagine Dr. Owen blushing with conscious pride, as he translated this borrowed gem. He implores the modest unknown to free his (Bacon's) name from the disgraceful part he had in the death of the Earl of Essex, and cries—

> "Oh, if I could
> I would make a willow cabin at your gate,
> And call upon your soul within the house....
> You should not rest
> Between the elements of earth and air,
> But you should pity me——"

Words full of passion and beautiful imagery when spoken by Viola, on behalf of Orsino, to the haughty and unresponsive Lady Olivia, but sheer drivel when taken as Bacon's exhortation to the discover of his wrongs.

But one travels in this precious cipher from foolishness to foolishness—from destruction to damnation, in quick, long strides. In the *Spanish Armada*, Elizabeth receives and answers the ambassadors of the King of Spain in the words that Henry V. employs in parley with the messengers of the Dauphin. She proclaims her physical superiority to her sister in the braggart language of Faulconbridge before King John beginning

"An' if my brother had my shape....
If my legs were two such riding rods,"

and the next dozen pages are a literal transcription of the first act of *Henry V*. A hundred pages further on we are introduced to Bacon's brother Anthony. The brothers meet during the progress of a storm—the storm that is described in Act I. Sc. III. of *Julius Cæsar*. The scene is placed in Dover, and Bacon who

"... never till to-night, never till now,
Did I go through a tempest dropping fire,"

happened in the streets upon

"A common slave," who
"Held up his left hand, which did flame and burn
Like twenty torches joined; and yet his hand,
Not sensible of fire, remained unscorched.
Against the *Citadell* I met a lion,
Who glared upon me, and went surly by
Without annoying me."

Bacon, in his normal moods, employs the royal style of "we" and "us" when referring to himself, but in moments of agitation, when, for instance, slaves and lions promenade the thoroughfares of Dover, he drops, instinctively, like a Scotchman into his native manner. "Whilst walking thus," he continues:

"Submitting me unto the hideous night,
And bared my bosom to the thunderstone,"

"I met foster-brother Anthony," who said,

"O Francis, this disturbed city is not to walk in,
Who ever knew the heavens menace so?...
Let's to an inn."

It might be thought that the foregoing instances have been carefully sought out and employed to italicise the foolishness of Dr. Owen's statement that the plays were first composed in this form, and that in this form alone is their true meaning and relevancy fully demonstrated. Such, however, is far from being the fact. If the reader will take the trouble to wade through the mass of incoherent commonplace, illuminated as it is by passages of Shakespeare's brilliant wit and inspired poesy which make up these five volumes, he will find scores upon scores of such meaningless and inopportune mis-quotations.

SHAKESPEARE AND BACON IN COLLABORATION. 69

THE BUST OF SHAKESPEARE AT STRATFORD-ON-AVON.

Dr. Owen himself concedes that "some parts of the deciphered material"—viz., those parts which have not their origin in Shakespeare, Spenser, and the works of the other masques—"are not equal in literary power, poetic thought, nor artistic construction to the well-known efforts of Shakespeare," but he accounts for this inequality on the ground that "the necessities for concealment were so great as to make the difficulties of the cipher serious, and artistic re-construction impossible." If it be granted, for the sake of argument, that the quotations from the plays, which appear in these "interiour" works, were from the pen of Shakespeare, and that the original parts are the product of Bacon, then Spedding's contention that there are not "five lines together to be found in Bacon which could be mistaken for Shakespeare, or five lines in Shakespeare which could be mistaken for Bacon, by one who was familiar with their several styles, and practised in such observations," is proved up to the hilt. Indeed, and without any such concession being allowed, it is impossible to compare the original lines with the pirated passages in these cipher books, and accept the two as the work of the same hand. Dr. Owen, who is evidently neither "familiar with the several styles" of Shakespeare and Bacon, nor "practised in such observations," invites his readers "to set aside the different names upon the title pages, and ask themselves whether two or more men could have written so exactly alike." His conclusions are equally destitute of logic or critical acumen: "Either Francis Bacon and William Shakespeare were the same man, at least so far as the writings are concerned; or else, for once in the history of mankind, two men, absolutely dissimilar in birth, in education, and in bringing up, had the same thoughts, used the same words, piled up the same ideas, wrote upon the same subjects, and thought, wrote, talked, and dreamed absolutely alike." It is true that Shakespeare, in cipher, bears an amazing likeness to Shakespeare in the plays, but if the Shakespeare in the cipher is to be compared with the Bacon either here or in his recognised works, Dr. Owen's conclusions are palpably absurd.

Dr. Owen promises still further cipher revelations of the same startling nature, which will explain how Bacon succeeded in using his various masques during the lifetime of the alleged authors. "In the decipherings which will appear in their regular order," he says, "I have found an epitome of the lives of Shakespeare, Marlowe, Green (he is probably referring to Greene), Burton, Peele and Spenser ... the circumstances under which they were employed, and the sums of money paid to each for the use of his name. Anthony Bacon, the foster-brother of Francis, was the unknown owner of the Globe Theatre. Shakespeare, while uneducated, possessed a shrewd wit, and some talent as an actor. He received, as a bribe, a share in the proceeds of the theatre, and was the reputed manager. Bacon, with his Court education and aristocratic associations, could not be known as the author of plays or the associate of play actors, and put Shakespeare forward as the mask which covered his greatest work."

THE TRAGICAL HISTORIE OF OUR LATE BROTHER ROBERT, EARL OF ESSEX.

EVEN at the risk of wearying my readers, it is necessary for the purposes of this book, to make a critical inspection of one of the "interiour" plays which Dr. Owen has deciphered from many of the principal works of the Elizabethan-Jacobean era. As all these hidden plays are derived from the same source—the writings of Shakespeare, Spenser, Greene, Marlowe, Peele, and Burton—the choice of a subject for consideration would appear to be immaterial. *The Tragedy of Mary Queen of Scots*, a "remarkable production," according to Dr. Owen, and one that "has been pronounced a masterpiece," would seem to have the first claim upon our attention. The selection of "*The Tragical Historie of our late brother Robert, Earl of Essex*, by the author of *Hamlet, Richard III., Othello*, &c.," has been decided upon, however; because, in the first place, it is a later production, and in the second, it is declared by Dr. Owen to bear "the impress of greater skill, more experience, and far more intense personal feeling." In the Publisher's Note, we are informed that it is "one of the marvels of literature," and "a work of the most thrilling interest and historical value." The prologue, which takes the form of a soliloquy, embodies "the deepest philosophy concerning things natural and spiritual, temporal and eternal." It can, moreover, "only be measured from the point of view of its author, Francis Bacon." This "wonderful prologue," which comprises some 200 lines of blank verse, is really a wonder of misapplied misappropriation. It opens with the Seven Ages of Man, to which Bacon adds an eighth, "which rounds out and finishes the story, with the "exit" from human view of all that is mortal:

> "Last scene of all
> That ends this strange eventful history,
> The old man dies; and on the shoulders of his brethren,
> To the heavy knolled bells, is borne
> In love and sacred pity, through the gates
> Of the holy edifice of stone, where, all in white,
> The goodly vicar meets them and doth say:—
> 'I am the resurrection and the life;'
> And then doth mount the pulpit stairs and doth begin:—
> 'O Lord, have mercy on us wretched sinners!'
> The people answering cry as with one voice,
> 'O Lord, have mercy on us wretched sinners!'
> Then through the narrow winding churchway paths,
> With weary task foredone, under the shade

> Of melancholy boughs gently set down
> Their venerable burden, and from the presence
> Of the sun they lower him into the tomb."

The "eighth" age, it will be observed, is not an age at all, but a funeral. To this striking addition to one of Shakespeare's best known passages, Bacon tacks on the whole of Hamlet's soliloquy, "To be or not to be," commencing with "To sleep, perchance to dream: ay, there's the rub;" helps himself to a pinch of Hamlet's lines, "Oh, that this too solid flesh would melt," acknowledges in the language of the King that "Our offence is rank, it smells to Heaven!" promises that

> ... "When our younger brothers' play is done,
> We'll play a comedy, my lord, wherein
> The players that come forth, will to the life present
> The pliant men that we as masks employ;"

borrows from Hamlet's advice to the players, and so—

> "The curtain's drawn. Begin."

The entire mosaic is the most unintelligible, inept, and exasperating mixture of pathos, bathos, and sheer drivel that has ever been claimed as the work of a learned, sane man.

The first act opens outside the Queen's hunting lodge. Elizabeth alludes to her hounds in the lines allotted by Shakespeare to Theseus (*A Midsummer Night's Dream*), and has an interview with the Earl of Essex, who comes to bring news of the Irish rising; and Bacon, who remains mute during the entire scene. In the second scene, Essex and Mr. Secretary Cecil come to open rupture in the presence of the Queen. Cecil cries, in Shylock's words,

> "Thou call'st me a dog before thou hast a cause,
> But since I am a dog, beware my fangs;"

and Essex retorts, in the prayer of Richard II.,

> "Now put it, *heaven*, in his physician's mind
> To help him to his grave immediately!
> The lining of his coffers shall make coats
> To deck our soldiers for these Irish wars."

In the mouth of King Richard II., these words had some meaning, for it was the King's intention to seize the possessions of old John of Gaunt after his demise, and Gaunt was on his death-bed. But Cecil is in excellent good health, and if he were likely to die not a shilling of his personalty would have reverted to the crown. If this was the original form in which Bacon composed the plays of Shakespeare, he was undoubtedly mad.

The Queen then administers to Essex the historical box on the ear, which so enrages the choleric nobleman that he "essays to draw his sword," and is summarily dismissed by the Queen, who, immediately repenting upon the reflection,

> "How bravely did he brave me in my seat,
> Methought he bore him here as doth a lion,"

THE TRAGICAL HISTORIE OF BROTHER ROBERT. 73

despatches Cecil to follow and bring him back. Essex boxes Cecil's ear, refuses to listen to his wife's reproof, and having sent for his brother, Francis Bacon (who greets him with

> "Brother, to fall from heaven unto hell,
> To be cubbed up upon a sudden,
> Will kill you" — —)

dismisses the smug, but "rightful Prince of Wales," and soliloquises—

> ... "But I'll use means to make my brother King;
> Yet as he, Francis, has neither claimed it,
> Or deserved it—he cannot have it!
> His highness 'Francis First,' shall repose him
> At the tower; fair, or not fair, I will
> Consign my gracious brother thereunto.
> Yes, he must die; he is much too noble
> To conserve a life in base appliances."...

Taken as poetry, or as logic, the effort is not a masterpiece; it is, presumably, one of those portions in which "the necessities for concealment" were so great as to make "artistic construction impossible." But it certainly explains, in a way, the reason of the traitorous behaviour of Bacon towards Essex in the hour of the latter's adversity. The poetry improves again in the next scene. By misquoting the words of Junius Brutus respecting Caius Marcus,

> "All speak praise of him, and the bleared sights
> Are spectacled to see him pass along," &c.

(it is impossible to determine whether the inaccuracies in quotation should be blamed upon Bacon or Dr. Owen), and adding thereto the jealous Richard II.'s contemptuous reference to Bolingbroke:

> "A brace of draymen did God-speed him well,
> And had the tribute of his supple knee," &c.

Bacon discloses Elizabeth's mental attitude towards the recalcitrant Earl. Directly Essex enters, however, the Queen promises him that he will soon be known as Duke of York, and she meets his objection,

> "My princely brother
> Francis, your quondam son, tells me flatly
> He is the only rightful Prince of Wales,"

with

> "The proud jack! 'tis true, if it comes to that,
> He is the Prince of Wales. But"....

Now Bacon must have known, as well as Elizabeth, that neither he, nor Essex, nor anybody else would be Prince of Wales unless so created by the reigning monarch. But Essex is so full of his Irish command that he overlooks such trifles, and in the next scene he sends a captain to the Queen for a thousand pounds, with the admonition,

"Be secret and away,
'To part the blessings of this happy day.'"

In the third act, the Queen does the sleep-walking scene from *Macbeth*. Essex returns to England, uttering the words used by Richard II. on his own safe arrival from Ireland, to be upbraided by the Queen in the Duke of York's words to Bolingbroke:

"Why have those banished and forbidden legs? &c."

A half-dozen lines of description (from *Coriolanus*) of Caius Marcus' return to Rome, illustrate the reception that London tendered to the disobedient Earl. Essex revolts, and fortifies himself in his house in London. When ordered by the Chief Justice of England to surrender, Essex replies in the magnificent curse which Mark Antony utters against Rome over the corpse of the murdered Cæsar. The lack of enthusiasm which the citizens of London display in the Essex rebellion is related to the Earl in the report which Buckingham makes to the King, of London's reticence in rebellion (*Richard III.*) commencing

"The citizens are mum, say not a word."

And when the insurrection dies out for want of fuel, he finds solace for his grief in quoting Richard II.'s lines—

... "Of comfort, no man speak,
Let's talk of graves, of worms, of epitaphs," &c.

The unsuccessful Essex in parley with Lord Lincoln employs the passage between Northampton and the King in *Richard II.*, and in the subsequent Star Chamber trial, the Chief Justice dismisses Essex to execution in the words that Henry V. applied to Scroop, Cambridge, and Grey:

"Get you, therefore, hence
Poor miserable wretches, to your death," &c.

But the marvel of inept plagiarism, of consummate wrongheadedness, and ignorance in the bestowal of stolen property, is seen in the last act of this marvellous play. Herein, Essex is discovered in a dungeon in the tower. He is a man 34 years of age, and it is somewhat of a surprise to find him declaring, in the (revised) language of little Prince Arthur (*King John*):

"So I were out of prison and kept sheep,
I should be merry as the day is long;
And so I should be here, but that I doubt
That *Cecil* practices more harm to me:
He is afraid of me, and I of him."

But it is more than a surprise to learn that this hardy man of war is to be compelled by Bacon (Shakespeare aiding) to play young Arthur to the bitter end. After being surfeited with Francis Bacon's choicest philosophy, the Lord Keeper arrives with a commission to deliver Essex to the jailers: "I will not reason what is meant thereby!"

It is impossible, without quoting the whole of this culminating passage, to

THE TRAGICAL HISTORIE OF BROTHER ROBERT.   75

convey a correct impression of the ludicrousness of the finale to this "marvel of literature," — this play of "most thrilling interest and historical value."

[*Exit* Keeper.]

First Jailer. Oh, he is bold, and blushes not at death.
Essex. Avaunt thou hateful villain, get thee gone!
First Jailer. There's the great traitor.
Second Jailer. Ingrateful fox, 'tis he.
First Jailer. Bind fast his corky arms.

Essex. Help, — help, — help, — help!
Here's a man would murder me. Help, — help, — help!
I will not struggle, I will stand stone still.

First Jailer. Bind him, I say.
Second Jailer. Hard, hard! O filthy traitor!
First Jailer. Give me the iron, I say, and bind him here:
To this chair bind him.

Essex. Let me not be bound:
Alas, why need you be so boistrous rough?
O I am undone, O I am undone!
Do me no foul play, friend!

First Jailer. Read here, traitor.
Can you not read it? Is it not writ fair?

Essex. How now, foolish rheume;
Must you, with hot irons, burn out both mine eyes?
O Heaven, that there were but a moth in yours,
A grain, a dust, a gnat, a wandering hair,
Any annoyance in that precious sense:
Then feeling what small things are boisterous there,
Your vile intents must needs seem horrible.
O spare mine eyes, though to no use but still to look on you!
Lo, by my troth, the instrument is cold,
And would not harm me — O men, if you will,
Cut out my tongue, so that I may still keep
Both mine eyes to see.

First Jailer. To see some mischief!
See shall thou never: (fellow, hold the chair:)
Upon these eyes of thine I'll set my foot!

Essex. He that will think to live till he be old,
Give me some help! O save me, — save me! — help!

(*They tear out one of his eyes.*)

Oh cruel! Oh God, — O God, — O God! my eyes are out!
Oh, I am slain!

First Jailer. My Lord, you have one eye left!

One side will mock another; th' other too.
Out, vile jelly! where is thy lustre now?

(They tear out the other eye.)

Essex. All dark and comfortless!—
O God, enkindle all the sparks of nature
To quit this horrid act.

First Jailer. Away with him; lead him to the block.

[*Exeunt Omnes.*

In the epilogue, the two jailers blackmail Mr. Secretary Cecil as he walks in his garden with his decipherer, and the book ends with the following cryptic lines:

"This is the cruel man (Cecil) that was employed
To execute that execrable tragedy,
And you can witness with me this is true."

(*Omnes*) "This is the strangest tale that e'er I heard."

This amazing adaptation of a perfect piece of dramatic writing to the exigencies of biography is, it may be assumed, without parallel in the history of literature. Comment would be superfluous: imagine Mr. Daniel Leno sustaining the part of Essex in a performance of the drama, and the illusion is complete.

BACON, THE POET.

The whole of the new matter that we find in the play under notice is so dissimilar from that of Shakespeare in style, language, and expression, that it might be the work of any author, American or English, even—if we accept the statement of Spedding—of Bacon himself. It is difficult to form any correct estimate of Bacon's talent as a poet, because, apart from his own description of himself as a "concealed poet," and his versification of the Psalms, we have nothing to guide us. Spedding doubtless had these Psalms in his mind when he pronounced so emphatically upon the absence of similarity between the writings of Shakespeare and Bacon. There is little extant verse of the period which is so un-Shakespearean as this product of Bacon's maturity, which was dedicated to the pious and learned George Herbert, whose verses on Bacon were printed in 1637. The publication is a proof that Bacon thought well of his work—it is not on record that anybody else has endorsed that opinion. Indeed, these seven Psalms give us all that we have, or want, of Bacon's poetry. The following is an extract from the first psalm:

> "He shall be like the fruitful tree,
> Planted along a running spring,
> Which, in due season, constantly
> A goodly yield of fruit doth bring;
> Whose leaves continue always green,
> And are no prey to winter's pow'r;
> So shall that man not once be seen
> Surprised with an evil hour."

His rendering of the 90th psalm is not all as bald and discordant as the following:

> "Begin Thy work, O Lord, in this our age,
> Shew it unto Thy servants that now live;
> But to our children raise it many a stage,
> That all the world to Thee may glory give.
> Our handy-work likewise, as fruitful tree,
> Let it, O Lord, blessed, not blasted be."

The beautiful 14th and 15th verses of the 104th psalm are thus rendered by our "concealed poet":

> "Causing the earth put forth the grass for beasts,
> And garden herbs, served at the greatest feasts,
> And bread that is all viands firmament,
> And gives a firm and solid nourishment,

And wine, man's spirits for to recreate,
And oil, his face for to exhilarate."

SHAKESPEARE'S HOUSE.

There can be no two opinions as to the merits of these metrical efforts, which Bacon thought good enough to print and to dedicate to his friend George Herbert. Spedding says of them, "In compositions upon which a man would have thought it a culpable waste of time to bestow any serious labour, it would be idle to seek either for indications of his taste or for a measure of his powers." And again, "of these verses of Bacon's, it has been usual to speak not only as a failure, but as a ridiculous failure; a censure in which I cannot concur. An unpractised versifier (fancy styling the author of the *Faerie Queene* and *Adonis*, an 'unpractised versifier!')—who will not take time and trouble about the work, must, of course, leave many bad verses; for poetic feeling and imagination, though they will dislike a wrong word, will not of themselves suggest a right one that will suit metre and rhyme; and it would be easy to quote from the few pages, not only many bad lines, but many poor stanzas." Spedding concludes with the comment: "Considering how little he cared to publish during the first sixty years of his life, and how many things of weightier character and more careful workmanship he had then by him in his cabinet, it was somewhat remarkable that he should have given these Psalms to the world." Dr. Abbott, another friendly biographer and admirer of Bacon's "magnificent prose," says:—"Some allowance must be made (no doubt) for the fact that Bacon is translating, and not writing original verse. Nevertheless a true poet, even of a low order, could hardly betray so clearly the cramping influence of rhyme and metre. There is far less beauty of diction and phrase in these verse translations than in any of the prose works that are couched in an elevated style.... But I cannot help coming to the conclusion that, although Bacon might have written better verse on some subject of his own choosing, the chances are that even his best would not have been very good."

But despite the appalling evidence of poetical incapacity presented by this versification of the Psalms, a staunch Baconian, by a train of argument which is only equalled by that employed by Mr. Theobald, has proved, to his own satisfaction, that Bacon was a poet, by locating the position which the Plays occupy in the scheme of Bacon's works. This ingenious logician has discovered that the two most extraordinary facts connected with Bacon's philosophy are (*a*) that the most eminent students have been unable to understand his "method of interpretation," and (*b*) that the last three parts of the *Instauratio Magna* are apparently wholly lost. Because Ellis and Spedding both declare that "of his philosophy they can make nothing," and that "he failed in the very thing in which he was most bent," therefore he must be a poet. Because the last three books of the *Instauratio* are "apparently wholly lost"—which is the writer's perversion of the indubitable fact that they were never written—therefore the comedies, histories, and tragedies of Shakespeare actually form the fourth, fifth, and sixth books of "the great work." Firstly (to present this argument fairly), Bacon declared his intention to insinuate his philosophy into men's minds by a method which would provoke no controversy; secondly (this is not exactly proved, but just stated as a fact), Bacon wrote the works of Shakespeare; and thirdly, the Plays are the treasure house of all art, science, and wisdom. The natural and inevitable deduction is that they must form the missing—*i.e.*, the unwritten—parts of the *Instauratio Magna*.

I am afraid that we must decline to accept so ingenious a piece of sophistry. Until it is proved that the Psalms are a forgery, or that they have been erroneously attributed to Bacon, we have a gauge of his poetical ability which is fatal to his pretensions to the authorship of the Plays, of Spenser, or of any one of the books which we are asked to believe emanated from his stupendous intellect.

"DID SHAKESPEARE WRITE BACON?"

Mr. Leslie Stephen, with amazing nerve and a fine sense of humour, has carried the war of the rival claims into the enemies' country, and propounded the theory, with no little plausibility, that so far from Bacon being the author of the Plays, Shakespeare was the real writer of Bacon's philosophical works. Mr. Theobald claims to prove that Bacon had ample leisure in which to write all Shakespeare and his own books as well. Mr. Stephen has come to the conclusion that his time was so fully occupied with business, and political and financial anxieties, that he never found the opportunity he was always seeking to perfect his great philosophical reform. Up to the year of the accession of James I., he had not been able to prepare any statement of his philosophic ideas. His desire, as we know from his letters, was to stand well with the King; his scruples, as we also gather from his letters, did not make him hesitate to employ questionable practices when he had his own interests to serve. If he had not time to write, he could get a book written for him. He selected Shakespeare, who at this period had a great reputation as the author of *Hamlet*, for the purpose. Why Shakespeare, it may be asked? Because, says Mr. Stephen, he knew Shakespeare through Ben Jonson; he knew Southampton as a friend and patron of Shakespeare, and he therefore employed Shakespeare through Southampton—the present of £1,000, which it is known was made to Shakespeare by his youthful patron, being money paid by Bacon on account, for the writing of the *Advancement of Learning*.

If the supposition that Shakespeare wrote this book for Bacon be correct, argues Mr. Stephen, "he might naturally try to insert some intimation of authorship to which he could appeal in case of necessity." Mr. Stephen sought for the intimation in the *Advancement*, and he discovered it in the first 81 letters. The opening words are, "There were under the law, excellent King, both daily sacrifices and free will offerings the one pro" (ceeding, &c.) These letters (to the end of pro) can be re-arranged to make the following: "Crede Will Shakespeare, green innocent reader; he was the author of excellent writing; F. B. N. fifth idol. lye." For the assistance of any one who cares to verify the cipher, Mr. Stephen explains that in both cases (the original and the decipheration) A occurs in 4 places, B in 1, C in 3, D in 3, E in 15, F in 4, G in 2, H in 4, I in 6, K in 1, L in 6, N in 6, O in 4, P in 1, R in 7, S in 3, T in 5, U in 1, W in 3, X in 1, and Y in 1.

THE CHANCEL OF TRINITY CHURCH, STRATFORD-ON-AVON.

Mr. Stephen assumes that Shakespeare explained this saucy little anagram to Bacon when the work was published, and that Bacon retaliated by "getting at" the printers of the folio after Shakespeare's death, and inserting a cryptogram claiming the authorship for himself. Bacon is imagined to have said to himself, "If Shakespeare succeeds in claiming my philosophy, I will take his plays in exchange." "He had become," says our theorist, "demoralised to the point at which he could cheat his conscience by such lamentable casuistry." In 1608 Bacon was Solicitor-General, and a rich man. He approached Shakespeare a second time with the object of having his great philosophical work continued. Three years afterwards, Shakespeare left the stage, and retired to pass the last five years of his life at Stratford. Why did he retire? "Because," says Mr. Stephen, "Bacon had grown rich and could make it worth his while to retire to a quiet place where he would not be tempted to write plays, or drink at the 'Mermaid,' or make indiscreet revelations." If it should be asked what he was doing, the answer is obvious. He was writing the *Novum Organum*. Baconians and Mr. Leslie Stephen are agreed that the *Novum Organum* is the work of a poet, and that it was written by the author of the Plays. But if it is conceded that Shakespeare wrote *Novum Organum*, it still remains a mystery to Baconians as to who wrote Shakespeare. After Shakespeare's death, Bacon, in *De Augmentis*, wrote that "the theatre might be useful either for corruption or for discipline; but in modern times there is plenty of corruption on the stage, and no discipline." Mr. Stephen deduces from this that in order to aim a back-handed blow at Shakespeare, Bacon would blaspheme the art of which he claimed to be master—that he was, in fact, according to our other theorist, fouling the fourth, fifth, and sixth books of his *Instauratio Magna*.

Neither of the theories we have just reviewed need be taken seriously. We know that Bacon himself gave an account of the scheme of the *Magna Instauratio* in a section of the *Novum Organum*, called the *Distributio Operis*. The fourth book was to have contained examples of the "new method," and of the results to which it led. The fifth was to contain what Bacon had accomplished in Natural Philosophy without the aid of his own method, and the sixth was to set forth the New Philosophy—the results of the application of the new method, and all the Phenomena of the Universe. Mr. Leslie Ellis tells us that Bacon never hoped to complete the sixth part; he speaks of it as a thing *et supra vires et ultra spes nostras collocata*. Mr. Leslie Stephen's whimsical retort to the *Instauratio* theory may be regarded as a *jeu d'esprit*.

THE CASE FOR SHAKESPEARE.

In propounding their theory that Bacon was the author of the plays attributed to Shakespeare, the Baconians rely on two main arguments: the plausibility of the idea that they should have emanated from the man whom Macaulay declared to possess the "most exquisitely constructed intellect that has ever been bestowed on any of the children of men," and the extraordinary unlikelihood that a man of Shakespeare's origin and antecedents should have written them. More recently, the disclosure of the bi-literal and the "word" ciphers, running through certain editions of the plays, and in Bacon's works, have placed a new weapon in the hands of Shakespeare's traducers. Already some of the supporters of Bacon's claims have assumed a sceptical attitude towards the "cipher speculations" — partly, I suspect, on account of their American origin — and Mr. A. P. Sinnett, whilst claiming that if the bi-literal cipher is substantiated, the Bacon case is demonstrated up to the hilt, hedges himself behind the assertion that the curious allegations now brought forward do not affect, one way or the other, the general force of the literary argument that supports the Baconian idea. But, unless a gigantic fraud is being attempted — which we have no reason to suppose is the case — Mrs. Elizabeth Wells Gallup's bi-literal cipher can easily be substantiated. When this is accomplished, we only get to the point that Bacon claims to have been the author of the plays put forth by all his contemporaries, while the conviction still remains, as it was expressed by Carlyle, that "Bacon could no more have written *Hamlet* than he could have made this planet."

It is interesting in this connection to briefly sum up the concensus of expert opinion that the leading scholars and students of Elizabethan literature hold on the subject. Mr. Sidney Lee, whose *Life of William Shakespeare* has been called "the most useful, the most judicious, and the most authoritative of all existing biographies of the poet," regards the theory as "fantastic." The substance of Mr. Lee's conclusions is that "the abundance of the contemporary evidence attesting Shakespeare's responsibility for the works published under his name, gives the Baconian theory no rational right to a hearing; while such authentic examples of Bacon's effort to write verse as survive prove, beyond all possibility of contradiction, that great as he was as a prose writer and a philosopher, he was incapable of penning any of the poetry assigned to Shakespeare. Defective knowledge and illogical, or casuistical, argument alone render any other conclusion possible."

Conveyance of House in Blackfriars, 10th March, 1612.

Mortgage of House in Blackfriars, 11th March, 1612.

The three signatures to the Will, 25th March, 1616.

1.

2.

3.

SHAKESPEARE AUTOGRAPHS

Conveyance of House in Blackfriars, 10th. March, 1612.
Mortgage of House in Blackfriars, 11th. March, 1612.
The three signatures to the Will, 25th. March, 1616.

Dr. N. H. Hudson, in his *Shakespeare: His Life, Art, and Character*, has on the Baconian theory four things to say:—1. Bacon's requital of the Earl's bounty (the Earl of Essex) was such a piece of ingratitude as I can hardly conceive the author of *King Lear* to have been guilty of. 2. The author of Shakespeare's plays, whatever he may have been, certainly was not a scholar. He had certainly something far better than learning, but he had not that. 3. Shakespeare never philosophises. Bacon never does anything else. 4. Bacon's mind, great as it was, might have been cut out of Shakespeare's without being missed.

But if, in the absence of anything bearing an even remote resemblance to proof, we find ourselves compelled to make a synopsis of expert opinion on the subject, we shall find no man's conclusions more deserving of respect and acceptance than those of the late James Spedding. Without intending to cast any reflection upon the critics and others who have plunged with ebullient enthusiasm into this controversy, it may not be out of place to point out that Spedding is head and shoulders above all disputants in knowledge, and second to none in critical ability. His knowledge of Shakespeare was intimate and profound, and he knew his Bacon more thoroughly than it has been the lot of any other man of letters to be known by his fellow man. He gave up his position in the Colonial Office, and declined the position of Under-Secretary of State, with £2,000 a year, in order to devote his whole time to the study of the life and works of Lord Bacon—a task which occupied him for nearly thirty years. Sir Henry Taylor, in a letter to a friend in 1861, wrote as follows:—"I have been reading Spedding's *Life and Letters of Lord Bacon* with profound interest and admiration—admiration not of the perfect style and penetrating judgment only, but also of the extraordinary labours bestowed upon the works by a lazy man; the labour of some twenty years, I believe, spent in rummaging among old records in all places they were to be found, and collating different copies of manuscripts written in the handwriting of the 16th century, and noting the minutest variations of one from another—an inexpressibly tedious kind of drudgery, and, what was, perhaps, still worse, searching far and wide, waiting, watching, peering, prying through long years for records which no industry could recover. I doubt whether there be any other example in literary history of so large an intellect as Spedding's devoting itself, with so much self-sacrifice, to the illustration of one which was larger still, and doing so out of reverence, not so much for that largest intellect, as for the truth concerning it." Sir Henry Taylor, in this passage, not only does justice to the diligence and genius of the author, but recognises the spirit in which the work was undertaken. Spedding spent thirty years in quest of the truth concerning this remarkable man, and having discovered it, he was prepared to maintain his conclusions with all the power of his knowledge and commanding intelligence. These qualities he exercised with paralysing effect against Lord Macaulay's *Essay on Bacon*. It has been claimed by one champion of Shakespeare's cause that Macaulay's "well-known depth of research, comprehensive grasp of facts and details, and his calm method of presenting honest conclusions, renders him pre-eminent as a safe authority." The exact opposite is, of course, the case, but the possession of these very qualities are revealed by Spedding in his *Evenings with a Reviewer*, to the utter spoliation of a great number of Macaulay's cherished calculations and conclusions. "No more conscientious, no more sagacious critic," according to G. S. Venables, "has employed in a not unworthy task the labour of his life," and the same writer has also declared that "the historical and biographical conclusions which he (Spedding) established depend on an exhaustive accumulation of evidence arranged and interpreted by the clearest of intellects, with an honesty which is rarely known in controversial discussion." Spedding is, in brief, universally acknowledged to be not only the greatest authority on Bacon, but also of the times in which he lived. His acquaintance with Elizabethan literature, its history, and its manuscripts was unique—he was, it may be said without fear of contradiction, a master of his period. "His knowledge of Shakespeare," says Venables, in the prefatory notice to *Evenings with a Reviewer*, "was extensive and profound, and his laborious and subtle criticism derived additional value from his love of the stage." The opinion of such an authority on such a subject as the authorship of plays attributed to Shakespeare is, in default of proof to the contrary, of the highest possible value—to a close student of Spedding it must appear incontrovertible.

Spedding's article on the question, which is included in the volume of *Reviews and Discussions* (Kegan Paul, Trench & Co., 1879) was written in reply to Professor Nathaniel Holmes' treatise on *The Authorship of Shakespeare*. In his opening sentence, he says, "I have read your book ... faithfully to the end, and if my report of the result is to be equally faithful, I must declare myself not only unconvinced, but undisturbed."

He is instant and decisive with his reasons. "To ask me," he continues, "to believe that a man who was famous for a variety of other accomplishments, whose life was divided between public business, the practice of a laborious profession, and private study of the art of investigating the material laws of nature—a man of large acquaintance, of note from early manhood, and one of the busiest men of his time, but who was never suspected of wasting his time in writing poetry, and is not known to have written a single blank verse in all his life—that this man was the author of fourteen comedies, ten historical plays, and eleven tragedies, exhibiting the greatest, and the greatest variety, of excellence that has been attained in that kind of composition, is like asking me to believe that Lord Brougham was the author, not only of Dickens's novels, but of Thackeray's also, and of Tennyson's poems besides."

Spedding, himself a genius, finds no difficulty in appreciating the quality of genius in Shakespeare. It was not scholarship, or environment, or training that enabled William Shakespeare to become the author of the most wonderful series of dramas in the world. Of Shakespeare's gifts, he frankly states the wonder is that any man should have possessed them, not that the man to whose lot they fell was the son of a poor man called John Shakespeare, and that he was christened William. If Shakespeare was not trained as a scholar, or a man of science, neither do the works attributed to him show traces of trained scholarship or scientific education. Given the faculties (which nature bestows as fully on the poor as on the rich) you will find that the required knowledge, art and dexterity which the Shakespearean plays imply, were easily attainable by a man who was labouring in his vocation, and had nothing else to do."

What Spedding failed to grasp was the difficulty which the Baconians find in believing that Shakespeare was as likely to be the author of the plays as any other man of his generation. In endeavouring to solve the extraordinary difficulty of the old theory of the authorship of the plays by substituting a new one, they have only made confusion worse confounded. "That which is extraordinary in the case," Spedding maintains, "is that any man should possess such a combination of faculties as must have met in the author of these plays. But that is a difficulty which cannot be avoided. There must have been *somebody* in whom the requisite

THE CASE FOR SHAKESPEARE.   87

combination of faculties did meet, for there the plays are; and by supposing that this somebody was a man who, at the same time possessed a combination of other faculties, themselves sufficient to make him an extraordinary man too, you do not diminish the wonder, but increase it.... That a human being possessed of the faculties necessary to make a Shakespeare should exist, is extraordinary. That a human being possessed of the faculties necessary to make a Bacon should exist, is extraordinary. That two such human beings should have been living in London at the same time was more extraordinary still. But that one man should have existed possessing the faculties and opportunities necessary to make both, would have been the most extraordinary thing of all."

ANN HATHAWAY'S COTTAGE AT SHOTTERY.

It may be contended, and with justice, that in the foregoing we have arguments that did not require the special knowledge and experience of a Spedding to prefer. It may not be, it probably is not, regarded by Baconians as serious argument, and, as Mr. R. M. Theobald would say, it would be simply a waste of time and words to discuss it. Certain is it that none of the pro-Bacon writers realise the necessity of answering, and, if possible, contravening these simple arguments. It is difficult to find any satisfactory reason for their reticence. But whether it is that they question the value of the views of the greatest student of Bacon on this subject, or are ignorant of his essay, or—what is more likely—are unable to combat so plausible a view coming from so eminent an authority, the fact remains that

Spedding's opinion is consistently disregarded.

It is not, however, that part of his argument which we have quoted, but the part which follows which carries conviction to those who are familiar with the work both of Bacon and of Spedding. The resemblances in thought and language, which are to be found in Shakespeare and Bacon, are accepted by Spedding as inevitable between writers nourished upon a common literature, employing a common language, and influenced by a common atmosphere of knowledge and opinion. "But to me," he declares, "I confess, the resemblances between Shakespeare and Bacon are not so striking as their differences. Strange as it seems that two such minds, both so vocal, should have existed within each other's hearing without mutually affecting each other, I find so few traces of any influence exercised by Shakespeare upon Bacon, that I have great doubt whether Bacon knew any more about him than Gladstone (probably) knew about Tom Taylor (in his dramatic capacity). Shakespeare may have derived a good deal from Bacon. He had, no doubt, read the *Advancement of Learning* and the first edition of the *Essays*, and most likely had frequently heard him speak in the Courts and in the Star Chamber. But among all the parallelisms which you have collected with such industry to illustrate the identity of the writer, I have not observed one in which I should not have inferred, from the difference of style, a difference of hand. Great writers, being contemporary, have many features in common; but if they are really great writers, they write naturally, and nature is always individual. I doubt whether there are five lines together to be found in Bacon which could be mistaken for Shakespeare, or five lines in Shakespeare which could be mistaken for Bacon, by one who was familiar with their several styles, and practised in such observations. I was myself well read in Shakespeare before I began with Bacon, and I have been forced to cultivate what skill I have in distinguishing Bacon's style to a high degree; because in sifting the genuine from the spurious, I had commonly nothing but the style to guide me. And to me, if it were proved that any one of the plays attributed to Shakespeare was really written by Bacon, not the least extraordinary thing about it would be the power which it would show in him of laying aside his individual peculiarities and assuming those of a different man."

There we have Spedding's reasons for rejecting the Baconian theory—let us summarise his conclusions in his own words: "If you had fixed upon anybody else rather than Bacon as the true author," he says—"anybody of whom I knew nothing—I should have been scarcely less incredulous, because I deny that a *prima facie* case is made out for questioning Shakespeare's title. But if there were any reason for supposing that somebody else was the real author, I think I am in a condition to say that, whoever it was, it was not Bacon. The difficulties which such a supposition would involve would be almost innumerable, and altogether insurmountable. But," he adds, "if what I have said does not excuse me from saying more, what I might say more would be equally ineffectual."

WERE SHAKESPEARE AND BACON ACQUAINTED?

IF we are to believe in the existence of the cipher, it follows as a matter of course that Bacon and Shakespeare were acquainted. Nothing is more probable. Bacon was at Court during the whole time that Shakespeare's plays were presented there. Bacon must at one period have been acquainted with Shakespeare's patron, Lord Southampton, who was the bosom friend of Bacon's patron, the Earl of Essex. Bacon was certainly in touch with Ben Jonson, Shakespeare's friend and co-worker. It is scarcely conceivable that the two most prominent figures in the literary world of the day should have been unknown to one another, although there is no authentic evidence to show that they were. In *Shakespeare's True Life* (1890), Major James Walter publishes an illustration of Bacon's house at St. Margaret's, Richmond, "where Shakespeare was a frequent visitor." "Twickenham," says the writer, "is a main connecting link with what is known of Shakespeare's visits to the neighbourhood; doubly interesting as clearly indicating his intimacy with Bacon, then living at his house, only a short distance on the other side of St. Margaret's, in Twickenham Park." Again, "It was just shortly before this plague fright, Shakespeare and Bacon had been jointly engaged in getting up one or more of his plays in Gray's Inn, and it comes with the saying they should be frequently together in the eminently charming retreat just acquired by Bacon at the munificent hand of Elizabeth's Favourite (the Earl of Essex)." "Catholic tradition," the same authority assures us, "asserts that Bacon wrote the first portion of his great essays under the cedars of Twickenham Park; others go further, and say our information is that Shakespeare and Bacon had a special fondness for the two old cedars, and spent much time on occasions of Shakespeare's visiting and resting with his friend at Twickenham, in reading and converse under the shade of these widespreading venerable trees." In another part of the same book we read: "Some families, whose past histories should afford information bearing on Shakespeare's life, assert that he met Spenser and Sir Walter Raleigh on more than one occasion at Richmond, and that Bacon was in the habit of receiving them together at his St. Margaret's home."

Interesting as are these details, they are, it will be observed, quite unsupported. What the Major says is, unfortunately, "not evidence." If Major Walter had given us chapter and verse for all this information, we might have verified his evidence for ourselves, but "Catholic tradition" and the unnamed "families with past histories," and the "others" are too vague to pin one's faith to. We may, however, assume that Shakespeare was not unknown to Bacon, that they met when

Shakespeare was appearing at Gray's Inn; and it is quite possible, if not probable, that Shakespeare consulted Bacon on the legal references and similes that we find in the Plays.

Bacon, although disloyal, and capable of shameless ingratitude towards his benefactors, had the love of his secretary Rawley, and the warm esteem of such men as Ben Jonson, Boëner, and Toby Matthew. Abbott, who is fully awake to his many faults, notes this curious inconsistency in his nature, and explains it in the conclusion that "whenever he found men naturally and willingly depending on him, and co-operating with him ... his natural and general benevolence found full play." If we accept this explanation, and it would appear to be the correct solution of his enigmatic character, we can readily understand that Bacon, in a patronising, but good-hearted way, would extend no little favour to a man of Shakespeare's position and reputation. Shakespeare would be familiar with Bacon's works, he may even have had the run of Bacon's library in Gray's Inn—an assumption of their intimacy, which, if supported by documentary evidence, would establish the theory that the poet used the philosopher as his model for Polonius. Bacon, the great philosopher, and the influential politician, would certainly have "the tribute of the supple knee" of all aspirants to literary fame. Authors would be proud to attract his notice, publishers would be flattered to allow him to glance through the proofs of any books that they were issuing. It is quite natural to suppose that if Shakespeare was known to Bacon, Heming and Condell would have been aware of the fact, and an offer to render them some assistance in publishing the First Folio would have been accepted with alacrity. Such an offer may have been made through Rawley, his faithful secretary; it might have come direct from Bacon to the publishers. How he obtained command of the proofs it is impossible to conjecture with any confidence, but if it is proved that the cipher exists in the Folio, and the other works mentioned—and I am satisfied to believe that it does, until a properly constituted committee reports that it is non-existent—it will be evident that somebody must have overcome the difficulties that the task presented. The law at that time recognised no natural right in an author to the creation of his brain, and the full owner of a MS. copy of any literary composition was entitled to reproduce it, or to treat it as he pleased, without reference to the author's wishes. Thomas Thorpe, and the other pirates of the period, were always on the look-out for written copies of plays and poems for publication in this manner. All Shakespeare's plays that appeared in print were issued without his authority, and, in several instances, against his expressed wish. How did Thorpe and his tribe obtain possession of the manuscripts of *King Lear, Henry V., Pericles, Hamlet, Titus Andronicus*, and the rest of the sixteen plays which were in print at the date of the author's death? If we knew for certain that Shakespeare and Bacon were on terms of intimacy, it would be a justifiable conjecture to suppose that the latter might have had a hand in the business, but if the existence of the cipher in these pirated quartos is verified, we may be quite sure that Bacon was the publishers' accessory in securing the MSS. for publication.

It is, however, more difficult to satisfactorily explain the claim of Bacon to the authorship of the *Anatomy of Melancholy*. The first edition, in quarto form, was

WERE SHAKESPEARE AND BACON ACQUAINTED?

published in 1621; the cipher appears in the folio that was issued in 1628. In the preface to this edition, the author announces that he will make no more changes in his work: "I will not hereafter add, alter, or retract; I have done." What do we gather from that, Mrs. Gallup may ask?—surely that Bacon felt his strength failing when he wrote those words; he certainly did not live to see the book through the press. But the fact remains that four more editions were published within Burton's lifetime, each with successive alterations and additions. The final form of the book was the sixth edition (1651–52), printed from an annotated copy given just before Burton's death to the publisher, Henry Cripps, who gained, Anthony à Wood tells us, great profits out of the book. This is one of the points upon which we shall hope to hear from Mrs. Gallup.

In this 1628 folio of the *Anatomy of Melancholy*, Mrs. Gallup has deciphered some ninety pages of a partial translation of Homer's *Iliad*. But on comparing this translation with that of Alexander Pope, written about a century later, it becomes clear that it is not taken from the original Greek of Homer, but is, in fact, a prose rendering of Pope's version. But Mrs. Gallup in a letter to the *Times*, which appears as these pages are going through the press, declares that an examination of six different English translations of the *Iliad*, and one Latin, shows her such substantial accord that either of them could be called with equal justice a paraphrase of Pope, or that Pope had copied from the others.

DR. OWEN'S WHEEL FOR DECIPHERING
THE "WHEEL" (IMPROVISED FOR READY REFERENCE), USED BY Dr. OWEN IN DECIPHERING SIR FRANCIS BACON'S CIPHER WRITINGS.

1,000 feet of canvas is covered by the pages of the works used.

IN CONCLUSION.

THREE of the main arguments which Baconians urge against the claims of Shakespeare to the authorship of the Plays are, firstly, that Shakespeare left no books; secondly, that only five of his signatures have come down to us; and, thirdly, that he makes no reference to his plays in his Will. When we come to investigate these objections, it may be said, without hesitation, that they do not amount to a row of pins. There isn't a rag of evidence, to employ Mr. Sinnett's phrase, to show that he left no books, it is quite certain that he left as much manuscript as Peele or Marlowe or any of the dramatists of his period, and it would have been something more than extraordinary if he had made any reference to copyrights which he did not possess. The professional playwrights of the period sold their plays outright to one or other of the acting companies, and they retained no legal interest in them after the manuscript had passed into the hands of the theatrical manager. When Shakespeare had disposed of his dramas, he washed his hands of them, so to speak, and not a single play of the sixteen that were published during his lifetime was issued under his supervision. They belonged to the theatre for which they were written. Shakespeare was only conforming to the general custom in this matter in betraying no interest in work which did not belong to him. He was consistently and characteristically indifferent as to what became of his plays, and in this he forms a striking contrast to Bacon, who had a mania for preserving and publishing every particle of his writings. In Shakespeare, this neglect, if surprising, is at least consistent; in Bacon it is too antagonistic to what is known of his idiosyncracies to be entertained for a single moment. Bacon must have realised that his versification of the Psalms was of less merit than the poetry in the plays. Yet he carefully superintended the publication of the Psalms, in the same year in which they were written, and kept no copies of such plays as *The Tempest, The Two Gentlemen, Measure for Measure, Comedy of Errors, As You Like It, All's Well, Twelfth Night, Winter's Tale, Henry VI., Henry VIII., Coriolanus, Timon, Julius Cæsar, Macbeth, Antony and Cleopatra,* and *Cymbeline*. These works of "supreme literary interest" were rescued from the dust-bin of the theatres, by the energy and affection of two of Shakespeare's brother actors, what time Bacon was translating his philosophical works into Latin, and publishing the Psalms.

In the foregoing pages, Bacon's character, and the incidents in his life have, it may be objected, been dealt with in a harsh and unsympathetic manner. Yet the facts set down are matters of history, and I claim for the comments, and the conclusions derived therefrom, that they are neither misleading nor exaggerated. It has been my endeavour to show that, while all that we know of Bacon's private life and his public career — the evidence of his deeds, his sentiments, his prose, and

IN CONCLUSION.

his verse—prove him to have been a man incapable of conceiving the poetry of the Plays, there is nothing in the life of Shakespeare, when freed of the miserable misrepresentations and baseless accusations introduced by his traducers, which makes it difficult for us to regard him as the rightful author. One thing we must recognise in the writer of the greatest poetry of all times—his genius. We cannot argue that Shakespeare had genius—and, therefore, he wrote the plays—but we may transpose the argument and declare that Shakespeare wrote the plays, and therefore he had genius. But, cries the Baconian, Bacon also possessed genius. The fact is incontrovertible. His genius inspired him to draw up the scheme of his *Magna Instauratio*, to write his *Essays*, to invent a new philosophy, and a most ingenious cipher, but it did not prevent him from composing some miserably poor verses or enable him to discern the singular absence of merit in his metrical effusions. There is not a single "literary" argument of the hundreds put forward in support of Bacon's claims to the authorship of the Plays which has validity, or even plausibility, to recommend it. There is not a single argument of the hundreds that have been advanced to deprive Shakespeare of his mantle which can stand the test of investigation. Carlyle declared Bacon to be as incapable of writing *Hamlet* as of making this planet. Spedding, who devoted thirty years of his life to the study of Bacon, emphatically asserts that, "if there were any reason for supposing that somebody else was the real author (of Shakespeare), I think I am in a condition to say that, whoever it was, it was not Bacon." We know that Shakespeare put the plays on the stage, and acted in them, and that his intimate friends, his fellow actors, and the public, believed him to be the writer. We know, too, that Bacon had a distaste, if not a contempt, for the stage; that his lifelong complaint was his inability to secure time for his philosophic studies. To sum up in a sentence, it may be said that there is no reason to suppose that Bacon was the author of the Plays, while there is every reason to believe that he was not; and with respect to Shakespeare, there is no reason to believe he was not what he claimed to be, and there is tradition, the testimony of all who had the best means of knowing, to prove that he was.

Until very recent times, one of the most tangible arguments of the Shakespeareans was that Bacon had not claimed the authorship of the Plays. That argument, if it has not now been thrown down, is, at least, suspended. The existence of the bi-literal cipher which Mrs. Gallup preaches, though vigorously attacked, has not yet been exploded. But if the cipher which contains these claims is verified, in the face of all circumstantial evidence that prove the claims to be baseless and preposterous, we are practically convicting Bacon of one of the greatest and most impudent literary frauds that was ever perpetrated. Yet that is what I am prepared to find is the case. Nor am I without warrant for holding this opinion. When the existence of the bi-literal, and the word-cipher has been acknowledged, we shall find that there are four other forms of cipher, the "Capital Letter; Time, or as more oft called, Clocke; Symbol; and Anagrammaticke ... which wee have us'd in a few of owr bookes." These ciphers are now being applied to decipher other messages which Bacon sent down the ages by this secret medium. Of the nature of these claims, I am, at the moment, unable to speak, but I am in a position to say that the contents are more sensational than any that have yet been revealed. The absolute proof of the authorship of the Plays is promised—but again we shall get no more than what Bacon considered constituted proof. In reality, it will form part of a gigantic fraud committed by one of the cleverest men that ever lived, it will disclose the flaw in "the most exquisitely constructed intellect that has ever been bestowed on any of the children of men;" it will prove, up to the hilt, the madness of Francis Bacon.

FINIS.

Lector House believes that a society develops through a two-fold approach of continuous learning and adaptation, which is derived from the study of classic literary works spread across the historic timeline of literature records. Therefore, we aim at reviving, repairing and redeveloping all those inaccessible or damaged but historically as well as culturally important literature across subjects so that the future generations may have an opportunity to study and learn from past works to embark upon a journey of creating a better future.

This book is a result of an effort made by Lector House towards making a contribution to the preservation and repair of original ancient works which might hold historical significance to the approach of continuous learning across subjects.

HAPPY READING & LEARNING!

LECTOR HOUSE LLP
E-MAIL: lectorpublishing@gmail.com

www.ingramcontent.com/pod-product-compliance
Lightning Source LLC
LaVergne TN
LVHW041604070526
838199LV00049B/2137